Beauty from Brokenness

Lessons Learned in the Storm

by Nia Hodge-Grier

Nia Marie

1 Peter 5:13-15

Nia Hodge-Grier / Royal Roots Publishing
PO. Box 4651
Fresno, Ca. 93744
sheskeepingitroyal@gmail.com

Book Layout © George Verongos

Editor George Verongos , Lauren Nefesha

Bible Verses are from the King James Bible or Hebrew Roots Bible or Strong's Concordance

Beauty from Brokenness "Lessons Learned in The Storm/ Nia Hodge-Grier. -- 1st ed.
ISBN 978-1-7337520-1-5

Cover Credits@ www.Canva.com

Dedication

All Praises to the Most High. Thank you for your love, mercy and continued favor.

This book is dedicated to the fruit of my womb, my 5 heartbeats. I love you with all that I am. To Maureka my Levite and the first to pass through my matrix, you have made me prouder than a peacock and I am so honored to be your mother. You are the first of many of my intentional choices. You are the manifestation of all the love I have in me with no restraints. I marvel at who you have become. A strong, intelligent, loving woman. I was blessed to give birth to my daughter and sometimes my teacher. You and your drive motivate me to push pass what my physical eyes can see and operate in true emunah (faith). You are truly my best friend; I love you pass eternity.

My dearest Allenique (Nuna), never would I have imaged that I would be expressing my love for you and you wouldn't be here to experience the next phase of Mommy's elevation. You have always been my biggest cheering section, believing that your mom could move mountains. You were my child who observed, so I was always challenged to be better because I knew if you saw me achieve it there would be no limit to what you would do. I miss the phone calls, "Momma where you at?" and "Gurl, guess what?"

You made me proud to be your mother. You were my sweetheart and my stick of dynamite. You and your siblings were always my reason to never quit in this journey called life. As I dedicate this book to you, I am eternally grateful for Yah choosing me to be your mom. I love you with an everlasting love. Thank you for my inheritance of the 3 Webbs, and my son-in-love Rodney.

To Michael Jr. my young king and quiet storm, keep praising Yah in your refining process and he will bring you on the other side as pure as gold. Some of your greatest setbacks were setups for greater things, believe that and know I love you.

To Isaiah, your destiny was foretold while you were still in the womb, line up with Yah's plan for your life and you will find out what real greatness is about on a higher platform. You are amazingly gifted and loved.

Karli, you are my sunshine. You are fearfully and wonderfully made. You are kind, sensitive, and smart, and I am so glad you belong to me. I pray Yah blesses me to see the gifts you have to offer to his kingdom. Thank you for being obedient and loving truth. Baby girl, stay compassionate and fearless and watch Yah use you and your gifts to encourage and lead.

To my grandchildren, my inheritance: Oshea, Jade, Michael, DeCorie, Rhyan, Tahje, Arielle, and Ha'sonn, I pray that this book will be one of many of the legacies that I will leave for you all to gain insight and wisdom from. To Rhikki Amarie Webb, the impact of your short time here was greater than anyone can imagine. Heaven is your great reward, and until we meet again, NaNa loves you.

Choose the ancient path which was designed by the command of Yahua. On this path you will find love, joy, peace, and comfort for the many sorrows this life holds. Remember, obedience is key to activate the promises of Yah. Obeying Yah and taking Him at His word is called love and having faith. Faith and obedience are how you will experience the Master of the universe.

Remember life happens in cycles and there is nothing new under the sun. When you have drifted far off or feel like you have lost your way, always look back to the beginning. In the beginning was Yah and he will not disappoint you.

Mom, thank you for being the vessel used to bring me into the universe. Love and honor are due to you.

To my only sister Monae, thank you for being my first best friend! I am blessed beyond measure to have a sister like you—kind, patient, loving, and always rooting for me whether I win or lose.

Thank you for being you, I love you more than you know.

To my Auntie Marcia, thank you for teaching me to delete daily and think on pure and lovely things, to always consider the arena I choose to engage in, and to count the cost of the decisions I make. Your wisdom and practical advice have made me a better woman. I have nothing but love for you. To the rest of my family, thank you for your love, support, and correction when I needed it. My tribe rocks!

To my circle of real ones, my ride or dies, you know who you are! I thank you ladies for being my safe place and sounding boards when I needed to process thoughts. You shared my tears and snatched my collar when I got close to the edge. I am blessed to have you all. Thank you for the prayers and loving rebukes. Your unchanging hearts and love toward me that never changed regardless of the ugliness I have revealed in some of my storms and transitions. I love you all beyond life.

Shalom and Simchah (peace and joy)

Nia Marie

Table of Contents

Foreword

"We journey inward." ~Yung Pueblo

I am the first to pass through the matrix of the author. Our connection is beyond time and eternal. I am the purest essence and intention of her womb, drawn out on a molecular level and birthed to stand witness in human form. Just as my connection to my mother is a witness, this book stands as a similar witness. I am the manifestation of her soul outward, and this book is the narrative of her journey inward. Bringing a book into this physical realm is similar to bringing a child forth.

Similar to creating a human in the womb a writer enters the scope of the creator. Fashioning and joining together both the light and darkness of lived experiences. She must separate the firmament of her knowledge from the waters of her travail to make way for a new life. When you read this book, you are taking a journey inward to a place where no man can go and where her and Yah dwell. This place is the womb of the subconscious and the soil of the heart. It is a garden space where to receive the fruit of one's labor; one has to journey through thorns, thistles, weeds planted by the adversary, and self to have what lies deep within.

My mother's story is one of experience, trial, and triumph. Her journey and path to the materializing of this work remind me of first fruit after a long sabbatical on a forgotten field. It is reminiscent of the restitution of Jubilee. Watching my mother write this work was like observing her prepare for the arrival of a long-awaited child. With anticipation, I witnessed as her metaphorical belly grew with the seed of experience, hurt, joy, and peace. I watched as she guarded, fought for, and prepared for this piece to come forth. I saw the opposition of the book in the wrong hands, I watched those who sought to distract to keep it from happening, I viewed the pain and anguish of the loss of my sister and the cares and stress of the world almost caused her to miscarry this project but all the while she persevered. Seeing how my mother guarded, obeyed, and walked close to the Father for instruction for this work was not only a beautiful experience but even more so an encouragement to all who are trying to become and stand in our truth in this universe.

This book is the first fruit of my mother, and I find a very intimate connection with this work. It not only gives insight to parts of my mother that I was not aware of, but it also allows me to peer into the life and the eyes of a woman who has seen and overcome a lot. Her story has given me insight into what it means to sacrifice. It has shown what it means to overcome insurmountable obstacles. It reveals what it means to pick up the pieces during a shattering and use them to express to a world the kind of healing that is possible at the hands of a master mosaic artist. Her story is the account of a continual blossoming. It is the narrative of soil that has born all kinds of fruit. She is good soil. It is a joke amongst the family that she is fertile myrtle, but I now know that it is not just the fruit of the womb that she can bear fruit from, but also, more importantly, she has been given a fertile heart. She is not afraid of weeding. She is not scared of the winter when the land lays dormant. She is not resistant to the pruning of the Master Gardener, and she always yields 100 fold. She has been faithful over her experiences and is more than qualified to stand before the eyes of the examiners with her fruit in hand to be judged.

I am writing this as a fruit from the soil of her womb. Growing up, I was told to take the good and leave the bad but what I learned over time was that even the things that seemed abysmal were on the exterior a graceful transparency for my growth. Each experience that I was allowed to share in was a testament to how each different nutrient and component came to existence in her lush garden. She is now freely allowing a broader audience to be nourished by her labor. I pray that as you read this book, it cultivates you. I pray that as you turn

3

through the pages and eat the fruit of the past and the present that you are nourished and filled with the goodness of the experience. As you read this book, I challenge you to take the tools of knowledge and apply them as the Infinite One leads you. As you push onward to your respective destinations, I pray that each piece of your puzzle and meaning for life is revealed from the inside out. I pray this book and my mother's journey inward is the companion you need for healing and that your yesterdays will make the reality of a better tomorrow tangible. May this book be a witness to others who are seeking to bring forth fruit deeply rooted in soil that is teeming with healing and wholeness.

–Maureka Davis

About the Book

December 18, 2018, I was sitting in the library trying to finish writing the last chapters of this book and meditating on a title. I was fasting and waiting on a word from Yah, praying for a new direction to take on my life's journey. I began to reflect over the last year of my life. I am living in a room in my daughter's house trying to reinvent a broken life. A life that had been affected by death, divorce, disappointment, and betrayal. I was emotionally disconnected and praying for a breakthrough. I was reminded of the scripture that says, "Yah will give you beauty for ashes." And the title of the book came to me *Beauty from Brokenness: Lessons Learned in The Storm.*

In this manuscript you will often see me use the name Yah, Yahua, Yeshua and Hamaschiac, Ruach qodesh to address whom many call God, Jesus, or The Holy Spirit. These are the original names used in Hebrew before the transliteration of the Holy Manuscript (Bible). I am a believer in truth, and I follow Torah meaning I don't only practice the principles of the first 5 books, but I believe in the Bible and do what it says. I keep and observe all of the biblical feast days and scriptures that I make reference to are from the inerrant word of Yah. Since I have returned to following the entire Bible as my point of reference and vowing to walk in obedience, Yah has allowed me to see my journey in this life through a different set of lenses and a new set of eyes.

Living in Torah isn't only done by reading but living in Torah is doing what you have read. True knowledge is the application of the education you have acquired.

This is for every woman who has pretended she was ok, when in fact behind the smile she was suffering silently. This is for the woman who has muted herself because she thought she was the only one going through a particular struggle and was worried about what others would think of her. This is for the woman who walked through the storm she was once afraid of and prospered. I have written this for the one who has always had to fight her own battles and set boundaries when all she ever desired to be was protected. This book is to encourage you to quit decorating your wounds with band aids and embellishments. This book is to remind you that our greatest disappointments and darkest days can be turned into motivation and healing. Remember, that in order for a house to be renovated it first must be torn down.

I thank you for choosing to allow my cadence on my journey to enlighten you on yours. I pray that you will use the principles that I have learned to facilitate you while you seek peace. My prayer is that after you are finished reading this book, you will evolve from seeing myopic to 20/20 vision. I believe the lessons and principles that I have chosen to share will enlighten and encourage you in whatever season of life you are entering or existing in. Life is cyclical and I pray that we will all meet at the mountain top together in due season. I pray that my willingness to be transparent gives you the strength to be courageous and discover that you too are beautiful and capable and courageous!

Lead, Love, Shine, Repeat!
Shalom and Blessings,
Nia Marie

Beauty from Brokenness

Pain is a Signal

"Before I was afflicted I went astray: but now I have kept thy word."

(Psalms 119:67)

Some of us have grown so accustomed to pain that we often get comfortable there. In some of our environments, pain was the only thing being served on the menu. One thing that reigns supreme is that pain can get your attention. Some of our pain tolerances are so high that a lot of us have become impervious to pain. Some of our trauma is epigenetic and generational. When I state generational, I mean that those who have raised you, passed their traumas and pain down to you. Epigenetic trauma is the theory that a person's life experiences, such as childhood trauma, has a biological impact on the way DNA is expressed. What you choose to do with pain and what it is trying to tell you is solely up to you.

I believe your pain is always calling you to examine yourself, and most of the time it is trying to save you from further danger and stop you from harming yourself, so that you can produce fruit and grow. You need to know how to respond to it and when not to react to it.

Pain can trigger some emotions that you thought you had dealt with but later find out you haven't completely purged. I have realized that emotions are very necessary and that they are gauges, but you should never let your emotions be your guide. I say that meaning don't let your emotions control your character and cause people to focus on your reaction instead of who you are at the core.

Who you are striving to be and where you are emotionally can give false feedback based on how you respond to negative and positive stimuli. This can also speak volumes of your character to spectators. People were created to be relational and communal and are looking for someone to model after. This should be something that we must remain cognizant of when we're working out our healing. Onlookers are observing how others heal so they can either model after them or avoid mimicking the way pain has manifested in the person. Becoming whole is work and someone is looking for the formula. When we decide to break generational curses, we are helping others to address pain.

In some instances, pain can act as a point of reference and can stimulate you to identify the root of your pain. I refer to this as the contents of your box being broken. When this event takes place, it is usually because the things being carried in your mind (box) have become too heavy to bear and the contents are spilling out. During this episode, you are faced with a choice. That choice is, "Do I pick up all of the things that caused the box to become too heavy and break or do I sort through the items sprawled on the floor and collect what is essential for wellbeing and wholeness?" Take into account that a lot of the junk collected as we journey through life isn't ours. The ideas, stigmas, and biases are usually things that were passed down or we just heard them rehearsed enough that we picked them up. As I previously mentioned some of our pain is epigenetic, environmental, and cyclical. Pain not handled correctly can send you on a downward spiral into the abyss of regret. When pain manifests, it should never be suppressed. Communities of color make up one third of the population in the United States. Most have been taught that therapy or counseling is for mentally ill or crazy people, or they lack the resources to receive the help that is out there for them. According to the Substance Abuse and Mental Health Services Administration (SAMHSA): "Communities of color tend to experience greater burden of mental and substance abuse disorders often due to poorer access to care, inappropriate care, and higher social, environmental, and economic risk factors." According to SAMHSA, when trauma has been mishandled or suppressed, the statistics show that pain manifests itself in multiple facets. Illegal drug use, alcoholism, and mental disorders. Sexually transmitted diseases can also be a factor when emotionally injured people are dealing with pain. There is no shame in exposing and dealing with pain. The shame and guilt come from trying to mask it. David, the psalmist and king in the Bible, referred to hiding sin this way: "Blessed is the man unto whom Yahua imputeth not iniquity, and in whose spirit is no guile. When I kept silence, my bones waxed old through my roaring all the day long. For day and night thy hand was heavy on me; my moisture is turned into the drought of summer. Selah. I acknowledged my sin unto thee, and mine iniquity have I not hid. I said, I will confess my transgressions unto Yahua my Elohim: and thou forgavest the iniquity of my sin. Selah." (Psalms 32:3-5)

Acknowledging pain, whether it was caused by your own choices or at the hands of others, is liberating and the first step to being healed. Stop subscribing to actions and thought patterns that perpetuate the cycle of pain.

Once you identify the root of your pain, stop going to the same toxic source looking for nourishment and care. You cannot get well in the same toxic environment that made you sick. There is a scripture that states, "If your eye causes you to sin, tear it out and throw it away. For it is better that you lose one of your members than that your whole body be thrown into hell." (Matt. 5:29)

Basically, remove anything and anyone that causes you to rehearse pain that you are trying to heal from. Don't allow traumatized people who choose not to heal facilitate you to stay in a cycle that isn't healthy. I have had the question often arise: "What if it's your parent that's the trigger of your pain?" Doesn't the Bible say, 'Honor your mother and father?'"

And I will answer, "Yes, however, the Bible also gives parents instruction on how to ensure that they will be honored. Ephesians 6:4 states: 'Fathers/mothers don't exasperate your children instead, bring them up in the training and instruction of Yahua.' And Colossians 3:21 reminds us also: 'Fathers/mothers, do not embitter your children, or they will become discouraged.' So, even if your parents haven't practiced the principle of not exasperating their children, they can be removed from your life. This should remain until they work on cultivating an environment that is conducive to healing."

Healing can only take place when you remove things that are a catalyst for sickness. Stop nurturing dead things. These boundaries should be set in all relationships, friendships included. Don't let your nostalgia cause you to continue to cultivate relationships that don't produce positive fruit either. It is ok to evolve beyond relationships that aren't healthy or only beneficial to the other party. The Bible states, "Be not deceived: evil communications corrupt good manners." (1 Corinthians 15:33)

"Do not make friends with an angry man, and do not associate with a hot-tempered man, or you may learn his ways and entangle yourself in a snare." (Provers 22:24)

My daughter and I have adopted a mantra that was one of my many quotes that the Most High gives me when I meditate on a lesson. The quote came as we were studying prayer (sound/vibration) and the laying on of hands and what that meant. Transferring energy and frequency. The quote is, "Your vibe attracts your tribe!" we put it on coffee mugs and a few t-shirts. However, it is true. Our attitudes, subscriptions to certain thoughts and behaviors, invites others that think or act the same way to desire fellowship with us. "Birds of a feather flock together."

So, find no error in elevating once you have been signaled that the place that your thoughts and emotions have been residing no longer fit.

Beauty from Brokenness

Pain Can Mar Your Reflection

As in water face reflects face, so the heart of man reflects man.

(Proverbs 27:19)

Pain has the power to cause you to lose sight of who you are. Meaning a lot of pain is rooted in our lack of identity of self and where we come from or knowing where we're from and refusing to change and grow. Growing up, and even now, we tend to get our affirmations of self from others or what others' perceptions and expectations of who we should be are. But identity is so much more than what others say you are or who you should be. It is essential in directing you on to the right path. If identity wasn't important why must we have documentation, such as a social security number, driver's license, or passport? Why, at a place of employment, do we need a badge or pin number to clock in? This is implemented so that not just anyone can say they are you and impersonate you or steal your identity. Our nation (United States) and other companion nations have really cracked down on documentation. The U.S. has gone as far as setting stronger patrols at boarders and here recently shut down the federal

17

government to get funds to build a wall to keep undocumented people out of this country. My thoughts on whether I agree will be discussed as I elaborate on this chapter.

Our point of arrival wasn't our decision. Neither was the region we would inhabit nor our language or color. We had no choice about who our parents would be, we didn't get to choose who our relatives would be either. All of this was by divine appointment and design. The environment we were raised in wasn't our choice either nor were the family values that would be instilled into us, as well so a lot of who we are was predetermined by others. However, the Master did allow us to come to be and protected us until we had the cognition to reason and understand that we can do better.

As a child, others were responsible for protecting you, teaching you and loving you. You probably were taught to listen and be respectful of others, to do what you were told, and hopefully you were taught to reverence authority and obey your elders as well. Whatever they didn't do in the small window of time they had you as a child is charged to their account and not yours, unless you still live in the past.

I see so many people bruised by their childhood experiences and it has carried over into adult life because their mirror still shows them a marred reflection—a reflection of a

18

part of them that is still broken because they haven't quite been healed from deep wounds that they never were properly treated for. The first truth that needs to be affirmed is that, as a child, you were solely dependent on another for your development as well as nurturing so what they did to you wasn't your fault, you were a child. They were adults and more than likely they were perpetuating a cycle that hadn't been broken in their life.

I am a firm believer of "when you know better you do better." You are responsible for only how you behave as an adult. If you have been blessed with the ability to discard the things in your life that give back a marred reflection, then your job is to do better than you were taught. Become what you needed when you were growing up.

If the values that were placed in you were solid, be fruitful and multiply them. And if the seeds that were planted in your life were negative and produced bad fruit, kill the tree from the root so that it will never grow again. I have witnessed people suppress and hide their truth and allow people who have inflicted injury upon them to control the narrative. They keep silent and suffer for fear of exposing and protecting their abuser. As if exposing the inflictor will make them look bad.

No, it won't make you look bad it shows courage in the face of what once scared you.

Again, in order to heal, some hard to swallow pills need to be administered. Some people never will understand what they did wrong if the person that was affected never shows them the err of their ways. And then you will have those that will shift the blame or never acknowledge their atrocities. That's fine, identify the offense give, the offender ownership to their own actions, and move on. When I say move on, I mean start seeing yourself through the lenses of love and truth. Jeremiah 1:5 says, "Before I formed you in the womb I knew you, before you were born I set you apart: I appointed you as a prophet to the nations." In this particular scripter the Highest is speaking to a prophet he was calling to be His representative and one to proclaim judgement to his nation. But we see there is someone who has a higher knowledge of us and has placed us in a certain place and time. The Most High knows the full garment of who we are and what our reflection should portray. "I will praise thee; for I am fearfully and wonderfully made; marvelous are thy works; and that my soul knoweth right well." (Psalms 139:14)

I have learned to heal by embracing the thought process that goes like this; I am not a victim! No, not as a self-

20

aware adult. I will no longer allow someone else's distorted views and actions to affect me. I am going to use the stumbling blocks cast in my path. Those blocks will help me build my sanctuary. We all need a protected place, somewhere sacred to meditate while we protect and guard ourselves from those who have wounded us or seek to harm us.

So many of us have been shaped by history books written by other nations and cultures of people whose main focus was to erase our identity and send us on a spiral of delusion and confusion. So many of us have been raised by descendants of slaves, with that being said, they have been indoctrinated and told who they were not and were beaten into submission. So, the only way they knew to convey information back to us about who we are is based on who they were told they should be. Since they were trained on how we should act some of our family members conveyed a really distorted perception of what our identity was, not based on truth of who we were before slavery.

Distorted visions and how we see ourselves has wreaked havoc on our men, women and children for centuries and injured generations of men and women, especially those who are the victims of the diaspora. The diaspora left us with broken families and nourished our people with regurgitated spoon-fed religions and doctrines and ideologies.

Due to this fact, we have lost sight of our point of reference, we have been catapulted onto a wild goose chase of lack of vision of self. And the largest number, by far, of victims of identity theft ever recorded and ignored. Isn't it funny that you can see things through distorted eyes because someone kept feeding you regurgitated relics? When, if you turn off your ears and observe things with your eyes you can see the real and what is true.

From a western thought perspective, we were taught that we were savages (the so-called Negro) but observation shows different, we were stolen, land taken, names removed, and ancient markers removed so that we couldn't find our way back to self-identity or home. "Do not move an ancient boundary stone set up by your ancestors." (Proverbs 22:28) This was the grandest act of deflection! A nation of people kidnap and sell humans into slavery and the ones being stolen and sold are called savages? A perfect picture of marred imagery? But praises to The Most High, we have advanced so much with technology and medicine that we are being identified and traced back to the people we were told were lost. "He will raise a banner for the nations and gather the exiles of Israel; he will assemble the scattered people of Judah from the four quarters of the earth." (Isaiah 11:12)

"At that time I will deal with all who oppressed you. I will rescue the lame; I will gather the exiles. I will give them praise and honor in every land where they have suffered shame. At that time I will gather you; at that time I will bring you home. I will give you honor and praise among all the peoples of the earth when I restore your fortunes before your very eyes," says the Lord." (Zephaniah 3:19-20)

Yes, their greed and need to display the spoils of war and tomb desecration has revealed that we are truly royalty but have been made to believe that we were paupers and fools.

We have also looked for identity in adults and our peers and various people that we grew up seeing whether they were a negative or a positive image. And as we evolved and became of age, we embraced images on magazines and pop idols on television that media, commercialism, and society said that we would try to see our reflection in.

A substantial amount of our imagery has been designed and created by other people, who have encroached and crossed other's personal boundaries. These people make themselves appear superior while making another group inferior. What I have stated may sound like a mouthful, however, I wanted to reveal the root of our strong self-delusion. Loss of identity is how we arrived at the place of seeing ourselves in broken mirrors.

When you have a false perception of who you are, you often believe others see you the same way. But life has shown me that others can see more of who you are than you believe you see about yourself because most of us spend more time looking outside of ourselves than inside. Once you realize that you are created, and the one who created you deals in original one-of-a-kind editions, it becomes easier to embrace who you are and find your place in the universe.

If some of us only knew how beautiful we truly are, individually as well as collectively, and that to your Creator, you are some of His best handiwork. We wouldn't stay past the expiration date of bad relationships; we wouldn't allow ourselves to be used or continue to make excuses for other's cruel intentions. If some of us realized how much love and thought went into the making of just one individual, we would rejoice. If some of us only understood that our Creator really got involved when He fashioned us. "Are not five sparrows sold for two pennies? Yet not one of them is forgotten by Yah. Indeed, the very hairs of your head are all numbered. Don't be afraid; you are worth more than many sparrows." (Luke 12:6-7)

He fashioned us with so much intent and purpose, so much so that he decided to document the day. On the sixth day of creation He stopped speaking things into existence and got personal and formed us from the dust of the earth and breathed life into His creation! "Then Yahua Elohim formed a man from the dust of the ground and breathed into his nostrils the breath of life, and the man became a living being." (Genesis 2:7)

Feel special now? I know I do, and this alone should cause you to quit looking at yourself in mirrors through broken minds and cease seeing distorted images of yourself. You were created with intent and purpose and in an eternal image. Then Yah said, "Let us make mankind in our image, in our likeness, so that they may rule over the fish in the sea and the birds in the sky, over the livestock and all the wild animals, and over all the creatures that move along the ground. So Yah created mankind in his own image, in the image of Yah he created them; male and female he created them." (Genesis 1:26-27)

I know it is easier said than done but it is very possible; remember, as a we think we become. That which you give power to has the power to master you and some of us have been looking in mirrors through broken minds and eyes for so long that we really don't recognize our own reflection. Our thoughts, or other's thoughts toward us, matter more than the truth about who we are—when I say "we" I am speaking from a woman's perspective. So many women have given so much of themselves to the wrong individuals that we render our cups empty. Our cups are empty from pouring out love, time, and giving undeserving people more chances than they deserve. We are left empty and with none to refill our cups. Here is where the lies come that we start to believe about ourselves. Because surely, no one would treat me this deplorable if I was just skinny enough, pretty enough, if my stomach was flatter, if I had longer hair, bigger breasts, a bigger behind. You catch my drift? Once we are rendered empty, we look for things to fill our cups up with to feel worthy. Not realizing that we possess the right components all along.

Confusion can lead to pain and pain can navigate you to places you never intended on traveling to. Places like resentment and despair. A club a lot of us have chosen to frequent is Pity Party and Blame Blvd. We do this to avoid accountability for our own actions. Or choose to wallow in pity because changing involves work and a real good look at self. We choose to blame others for not warning us that we were headed into a spiral of confusion and a lot of the people we have so often looked to for direction were lost themselves. One thing that is true and definitely for sure is, "The blind truly can't lead the blind and if they do, both of them usually wind up in a ditch." (Luke 6:39)

In all actuality, if most of us will be honest, we would not even have adhered to a warning if a warning was given. And most folks have had the warning but ignored it because the pain had taken over and became so loud that it began to cloud their vision. It also became so loud that it caused them to become deaf to truth.

When these two factors exist, it creates a smoke and mirrors effect and we begin seeing things totally different from the way they are. What we desire begins to become more important than what we see being conveyed to us.

Recently, biblical principles have started becoming more and more clear to me like Matthew 15:18: "But what comes out of the mouth proceeds from the heart and defiles a person, for out of the overflow of the heart the mouth speaks."

1 Corinthians 13:12: "For now I only see in a mirror; then we shall see face to face. Now I know in part; then I shall know full, even as I am fully known."

And as I grow older and things begin to fall into perspective more and more, I realize that there is a certain type of woman that I don't want to become, and some days I can see her getting dressed in her grave clothes and trying to emerge. She is the one who has looked into the perfect law of liberty and walked away and forgot what manner of woman she was. Anyone who listens to the word but does not do what it says is like someone who looks at his face in a mirror and, after looking at himself, goes away and immediately forgets what he looks like. "But the one who looks intently into the perfect law of freedom, and continues to do so-not being a forgetful hearer, but an effective doer-he will be blessed in what he does." (James 1:23-25)

I have been blessed with a solid core of friends, these are some women that have chosen to love me through my highs and lows. There was one particular instance where I was going through a very tumultuous time in a relationship and it was coming to an end. I was behaving so out of my character that one of my friends looked over at me and said, "I can't believe that someone so beautiful can behave so ugly!" Yes, hurt was the synergist for my behavior but those words caught my attention. I paused in mid-progression of committing a heinous act if she hadn't of interjected. I was driving and when I looked in the rearview mirror, the reflection that glanced back at me was a woman who had allowed anger from the lack of reciprocity in a relationship to almost drive her over the edge. Scripture reminds us of this: "Faithful are the wounds from a friend, but the kisses of an enemy are deceitful. Faithful are the wounds of a friend; But the kisses of an enemy are profuse." (Proverbs 27:6)

Moving forward, I began to reflect and examine my heart or sort through my box of spilled things, and some hard truths were revealed to me. I didn't see myself the way those who really loved me saw me. Through the eyes of some of my close friends, I was smart, strong and beautiful, and could do anything. But through my eyes and in my heart was a suppressed angry little girl who had to adult way before her time. She learned to enable, and she always felt like she had to perform and prove she was worthy of love based on the way she was reared. When she didn't perform according to the expectation of her parents, love was withheld. This manifested a silent rage.

I learned to suppress and convince myself that I was ok until triggered. That trigger was rejection, especially after I had loved and invested emotionally in a relationship and the person on the receiving end continued to take and not reciprocate. I have learned that just because a person wants you or likes you doesn't mean they are ready for you. "Can two walk together, except they be agreed?" (Amos 3:3)

It has taken me 27 years of my life to figure this precept out. I have realized that in order to resemble the reflection of your master and creator you must mimic and obey him. To operate the way you were designed, you must connect with the one who has the same components that are deposited into you, iron sharpens iron . The Most High created you to reveal to the world His image.

"Therefore, since we are surrounded by such a great cloud of witnesses, let us throw off everything that hinders and the sin that so easily entangles. And let us run with perseverance the race marked out for us, fixing our eyes on Jesus, the pioneer and perfecter of faith." (Hebrews 12:1-2)

I have been able to witness life happen to a lot of people close up and personal. One beautiful lady I thought I admired grew up sheltered and coddled. She was accustomed to getting her way and being taken care of and if she didn't get what she felt like she was entitled to, she would act out or manipulate to get her way. She was also fixed on portraying the persona of a perfectionist, so her outward beauty personified all togetherness. But when mistakes and continual poor choices were made, she refused to do the soul work. Others had taken care of her throughout her life and cleaned up her messes and gave her what she wanted but they forgot to teach her coping skills. When it came to introspection or allowing Yah to examine her heart and reveal to her where it should be fixed, she refused to make the necessary changes to make sure she would be ok. She chose to live behind a façade until it came crashing down like a dilapidated building and now she can no longer hide because the storm that was brewing inside has erupted on the outside and it's visible to more than just her mirror.

Having a front row seat to this unfortunate series of events caused me to examine my direction and where I could end up. I have realized that in order for you to heal, renovation is a process that has to take place at one time or another in life, and part of that process is that others will have to be uncovered if they were involved in constructing the original building that now needs to be rebuilt because of faulty wiring.

Know that it is ok to break cycles and to start over from ground zero in order to be ok is nothing to be ashamed of.

The Most High has revealed to me that the most important relationship and the source of identity came from an understanding of who He is. When I obeyed the first truth when His word was revealed to me, that's when I was able to see it manifest in the physical realm. The truths of Yah are functional and concrete and when you put them into practice you can see how real He is. "Let us, therefore, make every effort to enter that rest, so that no one will perish by following their example of disobedience. For the word of God is alive and active. Sharper than any double-edged sword, it penetrates even to dividing soul and spirit, joints and marrow; it judges the thoughts and attitudes of the heart. Nothing in all creation is hidden from God's sight. Everything is uncovered and laid bare before the eyes of him to whom we must give account." (Hebrews 4:11-13)

Obeying simple universal laws will unlock truths to principles and allow you to apply them to your life for change and growth.

What's on the inside eventually will manifest in word, in deeds and finally in actions. It's inevitable that what goes in comes out. That's why you can hear a person's actions louder than they can ever speak to you.

I see what I like to refer to as the *backwards mirror ministry*. This is when we keep the back of the mirror facing ourselves and the part that reflects pointing at others while we deflect all of our faults on them and fail or refuse to see our own flaws. Another term for this behavior is internal conflict or cognitive dissonance. They have become masters of disguise and experts at excusing away what they see.

Some people cannot handle what's going to be revealed by truth and mirrors that they didn't create in their minds, and this is why they live in this secluded world called denial. So, people choose to go through life wearing camouflage to cover up pain thinking it won't be exposed, but when the rain and elements of life happen, what's underneath will show because water washes away disguises and paint. The power of truth can wash and heal broken and scarred emotions, but most aren't willing to let the water of the word of truth penetrate their hearts.

The question is do you know what you really look like? Are you caught up in the society of idols and illusions, symbols and media? Do stars and commercials and messages that media uses to persuade you of what we should look like and how we should behave lead you astray?

We mimic how other people behave or try to live up to personas that others have nurtured in our lives so we believe we should behave or continue to mimic an ideology so that we can look like we belong. I have realized that no amount designer gear, makeup, cars or material items can cover up pain. I don't care how many websites sell fake purses, fake hair, make up, shoes or even identities; when that all comes off, what reflection do you see when you look in the mirror? Is it that little girl that was never encouraged while she was growing up? Is it that little girl that was made to believe that she had to perform for love because the parents were unavailable or too engulfed in their own pain to show affection?

Is that the injured little girl whose father was absent, and she never saw what it looked like for a man to really love a woman, so she keeps finding herself in meaningless hurtful relationships?

If any of these references made apply to your situation, there is a prescription, and you can be healed. I used to believe that holding on to hurt made me strong, but it just created a high pain tolerance and made me tired. It was letting go that actually gives you more strength and the ability to help carry others over the threshold to heal.

People see the real you by the words you use, the company you keep and the actions you display. Eventually, you will be tried by fire and if you are full of impurities, then the fire will reveal this and if there are precious metals and genuine qualities that can be put on display for others to marvel at, it will be revealed. Take the time to see what you are made of by deciding to keep it real where you have to live at. Healing needs to be holistic consisting of your mind, body, and soul. Quit following false images and quit living a life that causes you to keep drifting further into darkness. Remember, you were created to be an ambassador and guide to point others in the direction of the Creator.

Your reflection is evidence of what is going on inside, spiritually as well as what is taking place mentally and physically in your life. And reflections become marred the moment we exchange what is true for what is a lie. When we embrace a lie instead of continuing in truth, we spiral into an identity crisis.

The enemy can only speak and make suggestions that appease our desire and our senses, but he needs you to act on his persuasive speech because without a vessel he can't act in the physical realm. Our enemy uses the past hurts as well as idols, illusions, and symbols coupled with false messages to keep us blind to the image we display.

The moment you agree to participate in a lie, you pledge allegiance to the dark side, and whether you will admit it or not, whoever you obey is your master, whether it is your feelings, your friends, your emotions, or media. It becomes hard to tell the counterfeits from the fake when the only template you have to measure up to is a cracked reflection. A lot of us follow cracked reflections because the picture looks pretty on social media, Instagram, Facebook and Snapchat. Focusing on other's reflections helps many not deal with their own lives and if their lives are good, believe me, it didn't come easy—it takes work and repair to have peace and joy. Money may buy a good time, but peace and joy are priceless.

Again, a marred reflection is created when we try to measure up or compare ourselves to the object that we believe is the real source of love. Remember we need to take a look at what love is and then apply it to our lives as well as our deeds. The perfect example of love is that "Love is patient, love is kind and is not jealous. Love does not brag and is not arrogant, it does not act unbecomingly, it does not seek its own way; it is not provoked, does not take into account a wrong suffered and does not rejoice in unrighteousness but rejoices the truth." (1 Corinthians 13:4-6) Some of us have operated in pain so long that we don't know we are broken. The pain has made us paint and hide our faces behind masks, makeup, and fake friends with fake smiles.

Women's hearts are a deep ocean of secrets and as we live, we become masters of covering up. But real wisdom and beauty comes from above; truth may hurt with the first cut, but it only hurts when it's cutting at a lie. Truth can even seem crazy if you're not used to hearing it as well, but once you begin operating in truth, you won't settle for anything less than the foundation of truth; this is the place where strong women are built.

Thank you, Yah, for the perfect mirror that will showcase a beautiful reflection and has the power to give us liberty and free us from the scars we have received from living in bondage and darkness. That mirror is the perfect word of our creator. Who do you see when you look in your mirror? What does your mirror reflect? Live, love and shine my Sister!

Beauty from Brokenness

Loving and Being Loved

"There is no fear in love, but perfect love drives out fear: because fear hath torment. He that fearth is not made perfect in love."

(1 John 4:18)

The unknown can be intriguing and often scary, it can lead to some very paralyzing thoughts and behaviors if we obsess about it too long. If it's really love, it will light your path to take the next step into the unknown.

Obsessing is real and we can become a prisoner to our thoughts if we wonder about the what-ifs all the time and for too long. I was once told that what-ifs are lies because they haven't happened yet. What-ifs are the action of false evidence appearing real that you have given power over your thoughts and everyday life and they can begin to paralyze you and inhibit you from experiencing real love and joy in this life.

We don't know what the future holds, nor do we know how others will feel about us. In the end the only things we have control over are ourselves and our emotions, meaning who we allow in our lives and how we decide to respond to stimuli around us is the most important element in life.

Loving involves a lot of unknown variables, such as when we love, there is no guarantee that the person or the people we love are going to love us back. Second, we cannot guarantee that they won't leave. When you love, there is a possibility that the person may decide they don't love you anymore or they may leave involuntarily meaning they may pass away. They may pretend to know how to love you and sooner or later their true colors may reveal that they were putting up a façade just to gain a vulnerable place in your heart to hurt you. Whatever the case may be, I have witnessed that most people lack the ability to demonstrate true reciprocity. Meaning most seem to repay your good with ill intentions and deeds. They are given real love but don't know how to return it.

Sometimes, the object of your affection reciprocates and sometimes you are left picking up the many pieces of your broken heart. Sounds like gambling? Maybe! However, you will never know what good is unless you have experienced bad and vice versa.

Does this mean you never have another conversation with a person of the opposite sex or consider a companion? I will say, "no!" But to keep succumbing to vain encounters can produce anxiety. My advice is to make sure the person has substance and observe their actions and conversations.

Words lie but actions rarely do, "Vibes don't lie," stay vigilant. Each time we encounter a good or bad experience we are challenged to glean from that situation and to elevate and perform for a better outcome and do so to a higher standard if/when the situation presents itself again. Life isn't to be lived in fear and love is what we were created for. We were created to have fellowship with Yah and out of fellowship, comes relationship, and when you know that you can trust a person, love is the outcome.

You may not know how to read minds but most people who are interested in you or vibing with you will speak their intentions toward you if you ask, and sometimes this is done without you inquiring.

You won't have to wonder too long about their words because their actions and tone toward you won't ever lie. If their words aren't matching their actions toward you then they are a liar and this kind of love is scary. When we try to force what we experience to mean or be interpreted as something else other than what it is, we see. If a man is unfaithful to you that means just what it says... he can't be trusted! If he hits you that means he is violent. Not, "He loves me." See, it's plain. If he lies to you, he is a liar. Not, "He didn't want to hurt my feelings." He is just trying to protect his own interests with the lie. This kind of love is toxic and scary when you try to make it something it's not… a big mess.

See, we have this idea of the package love is supposed to come wrapped in and if it doesn't look tall enough, gangsta enough, fine enough, or rich enough we don't unwrap it and 9 out of 10 times, this is where we miss out on love and end up trying to do magic.

We try to make someone who lacks all of the attributes and ingredients that generate real love, love on us.

As a newborn child, you don't have any inhibitions about crying when you are hungry, wet, lonely or wanting to be swaddled. So, to feel secure or have your needs met you just expressed your desires by crying out and the one who gave birth to you nurtured you.

Now, I understand some people's arrival and journey may have been different, but I'm speaking in general and assuming that most can relate to what I am referring to. At birth, you didn't know to suppress or obsess about loving your parents, siblings or family, you just did and did it without all of the frantic thoughts about what if they don't love me back?

What if they leave? What if they hurt my feelings? What if they lie? All of these fears were taught either by experiencing those emotions or by someone indoctrinating you with the thought.

The unknown can be quite intriguing and frightening; however, every day is unknown, we don't know what is on the other side of a sunset, all we know is tomorrow will come.

What I have learned to be true is that we can choose, as we mature and start to walk life's journey with adults who we allow into our space. Love should sanctify you and make you better not bitter and fearful. "Treat younger men as brothers, older women as mothers, and younger women as sisters with absolute purity." (1 Timothy 5:2)

If we embraced these principles, there would be a lot less hurt going on between male and female relationships. In living and loving we never truly know what our expected end will be, but we do know that we are not here without a list of instructions, we just have to follow them. "All scripture is given by inspiration of God, and is profitable for doctrine, for reproof, for correction, for instruction in righteousness." (2 Timothy 3:16)

Love isn't a mystery, we just choose to accept the wrong love from people and then become afraid that what we have grown accustom to is the only thing everyone else knows how to do too.

"This is love; Greater love has no one than this: to lay down one's life for one's friends." (John 15:13)

This literally tells you that love protects and is willing to do so with one's own life. If a person is willing to do this, there is no question about whether they adore you or not.

This type of love isn't a mystery either: "You shall not hate your brother in your heart, but you shall reason frankly with your neighbor, lest you incur sin because of him. You shall not take vengeance or bear a grudge against the sons of your own people, but you shall love your neighbor as yourself: I am Elohim" (Leviticus 19:17,18) (Loving your neighbor as yourself can be seen in vs. 9-18 of Leviticus)

To exist in the same vicinity as another and to mistreat them isn't considered love; that is cruel and hateful. See, love isn't hard to decipher when you use the Bible as your point of reference.

Last, this is the template on how to love a person that has exemplified all the attributes of a person that loves you. We are never called by our creator to endure mental or physical abuse at the hands of our mates, parents or so-called friends; it is a direct contradiction to his very words, we are supposed to reciprocate and demonstrate the same love that he exemplifies to us.

This only demonstrates to us that the type of love we should accept should be no less than sacrificial, selfless, and protective. I have stated earlier that the word of our creator is functional as well as the language that he chose to speak the world into existence with. Love is how Yah personifies who he is. "Thus saith Yahua, The people which were left of the sword found grace in the wilderness; even Israel, when I went to cause him to rest. Yahua Elohim hath appeared of old unto me, saying, Yea, I have loved thee with an everlasting love: therefore with loving kindness have I drawn thee." (Jeremiah 31:2-4)

"So shall my word be that goeth forth out of my mouth: it shall not return unto me void, but it shall accomplish that which I please, and it shall prosper in the thing whereto I sent it." (Isaiah 55:11)

This is the same evidence our love should exemplify being that we are created and exist to glorify our Creator. The word love in Hebrew is Ahava. I will give you a few of the meanings here and for those of you who study the Bible, I will leave a reference tool so that you can see the many functions of love. Love is an action word and if there are no actions behind a person saying they love you; it very well may just be gas! The functions of love are this: relating intimately, providing for the house, conforming or being agreeable. Love also functions in this capacity: it acts as a refuge, protection and hides or covers. Love protects from harm, empathizes and watches the one it loves as well as knows the thoughts and intentions toward the object of their affections. The intentions are to never hinder nor harm the loved one. Neither to bring them shame.

"For I know the thoughts that I think toward you, says the Lord, thoughts of peace and not of evil, to give you a future and a hope." (Jeremiah 29:11)

Ahav (AHB) Strong's #157,160,1090,/AHLB#1094 , (Rahh)#7453, 7462, 7470, ABLH# 1453, #7356,-60/AHLB #2762

Sometimes We Choose Pain

"When tempted, no one should say, 'Yah is tempting me.' For Yah cannot be tempted by evil, nor does he tempt anyone; but each person is tempted when they are dragged away by their own evil desire and enticed. Then, after desire has conceived, it gives birth to sin; and sin, when it is full-grown, gives birth to death."

(James 1:13-17)

From personal experience, I can attest to the fact that I have never believed a lie I didn't want to be true. Situations that really weren't ideal or healthy that I participated in were because I wanted to. I believe everyone should know themselves enough to say what they like or dislike. You should know enough about yourself to know what you will and will not accept.

To put it in layman's terms, every woman should have a mission statement, a mantra of who she is, and she should with every fiber of her existence not be moved or persuaded from the truths that make her a woman. Unless they are less than the moral standard. Meaning, if they are harmful to others, disrespectful to Yah or her family and don't edify other sisters. That statement should involve truths that she has learned about herself and she is unapologetic for standing on them. This mission statement should be a boundary and once these things are crossed you should have an exit plan for the situation.

Just as our creator has given us commandments and instructions to live by, which creates a covenant and strong relationship with him, when we adhere to them. We bring him (Yahua) honor and glory when we abide in his commandments and he provides protection, peace and blessings for us when we obey him.

"The people all responded together, 'We will do everything the Yahua Elohim has said.' So Moses brought their answer back to the Yahua." (Exodus 19:8) "And Yahuah said, 'Behold, I am making a covenant. Before all your people I will perform wonders that have never been done in any nation in all the world. All the people among whom you live will see Yahua's work, for it is an awesome thing that I am doing with you. Observe what I command you this day. I will drive out before you the Amorites, Canaanites, Hittites, Perizzites, Hivites, and Jebusites...." (Exodus 34:10-11)

If our creator has implemented laws and boundaries that if broken cause discord in our relationship with him then we should also. After all, we are to mimic the one that we say we put our trust in and follow. In ancient Hebraic customs, when two people entered into a covenant, a chosen and fitted animal was picked to be sacrificed. This animal was without spot or blemish, the not sick or a throw away animal. This animal would be worth a lot of money if it was sold, therefore costing the one sacrificing it something. The animal was then severed or cut in two in order to permit the two parties to pass through the divided animal. This was done to signify the bond and also to show an example of what the consequence would be for breaking the covenant. Once the covenant was established, just as the animal was split into two, breaking the agreement (covenant) would produce the same result for the one who broke the covenant.

In a relationship when a set of non-negotiables or intentions are discussed before the relationship begins and if they are broken, this breaks the covenant and kills components of the relationship. This is relevant in different types of relationships from friendships to marriage. Lying, divulging private information and cheating, breaks the most important component of a relationship....Trust!

I remember reading a quote a young lady had written on social media; she was asking how she got to this place in her life again. She asked, "Why aren't there bread crumbs placed on this path to lead me back on the right trail when I stray too far? How had she ending up disappointed, hurt and rejected again?" After reading her quote, I wished that her pain and insatiable need to be wanted wasn't so loud that she could have heard the lies that were being told to her by the person that she was infatuated with at the time. She was looking for breadcrumbs, but she ignored the red flags. There had been a substantial amount of red flags waving that would have alerted her to the other party's behavior. A long list of repeat offenses and collateral damage had been left behind. At the time the lies that she wanted to be true overrode the evidence before her. The red flags were there to direct her away from pain, but she couldn't identify them because she was lost and hungry for love. She wanted to experience love or what she thought was love and didn't care that the party involved was a married man. It is a true statement that hurt people hurt other people, and in her attempt to get solace and validation for her desires, she participated in the act of defiling the marriage bed. A child would be born from this encounter. After the child was born, the female couldn't believe that the person who broke the covenant he had went into with another person, would refuse to engage with her and her child. When all along the man's lack of loyalty and integrity were present.

People who don't have a mission statement will write the rules as they go only to realize the entire universe was created to operate on principles. One of the principles is called reciprocity. Reciprocity can be beautiful when it operates as it was designed to, and it can be painful, as painful as falling off your bike into a thorn bush when you are trying to make it function on your own will and desires. The first component needed for reciprocity to work is an open fertile heart and mind.

Romans 1:20 says that the earth bears witness of the creator. The same is true when we look at how some people's lives bear visible evidence of the results of their choices.

She believed the man would be faithful to her while cheating on his wife. The evidence to her truth was being performed right before her eyes, but she chose to put on rose-colored glasses. That didn't make the reality less than true, it just added a colorful perspective. Like I said before, the universe was created on a principle called reciprocity. You only have to plant one seed for a whole tree to grow, in this instance a seed was planted, and a life was born. Acts of sin manifest visual testaments of the things we participated in; life isn't a sin but some of the events leading up to it life manifesting have some colorful stories behind them.

Because of the lack of having a mission statement, they want others to participate in the fruit of their hands with no perspective or objections to the dark behaviors that took place. But when you analyze this type of behavior, you are asking for followers and not friends, a friend loves at all times but will also give you loving rebuke. This rebuke doesn't have to be public and no one has to know how the friend dealt with you and the behavior, but these kinds of situations always make a real friend wonder if they are exempt to your out of control desires. The way some women envision in their minds how folly and foolish situations should be handled isn't quite like the plan they have mapped out in their head. Instead of oohs, ahhhs and lavish gifts, they receive questions, distance, side eyes and disdain. We often ask for a sign to show us whether or not a person can be faithful or if the person is for us but then ignore all of the observational evidence. We try to manipulate the evidence to make it fit the desires we have and find ourselves in a lot more hurt than we had prepared to deal with. Most of us choose based solely on what we believe we want. And if we are truthful, we choose situations to involve ourselves in based on what we think we believe we can handle.

Usually, the same way we start a situation is the way the situation will end. If we start out with lies and deceit that is how it will end. If we built a house without a solid level foundation the frame won't stand, eventually it will collapse and after you clear the rubble what's left to salvage will show what that house was made of and what it lacked.

This is the law of reciprocity. Plant pain and watch and witness how it multiplies and transfers like a wildfire. The same principle is true with love and that's why a lot of our griefs come from the acceptance of tainted love and then we wonder why we get the same kind back. Most of mankind's desire for love comes from a pure place, but many don't know how to love the way others desire to be loved.

Now, because of your desire for love and to receive it back, we make questionable choices and innocent people are affected by it. You can nudge people into your pool of pain because you thought you could deal with it; the choice prompted by your desires that only involved satisfying your need to receive. This is the principle of reciprocity but not quite how you saw it in your mind. Then once the pain is administered like a lethal dose of medicine, you tell yourself, "I thought I could handle the consequences."

Most of us have watched movies like *Back to the Future* and the *Butterfly Effect,* and if you remember in these movies, certain things had to be done an exact way when the people traveled back in time or they affected the course of the future thus disrupting certain elements in the universe.

Let's take a history lesson and see if this is true. Abraham was told to leave the land of his father and follow Yahua and if he followed Yahua that he would make a great nation out of him. He promised him a seed from his own loins with his wife because his wife's womb was barren. This was solidified by Yah making a covenant with Abram. "Yah said, 'Bring me a heifer, a goat, and a ram, each three years old, and a dove and a young pigeon.' He brought all these animals to him, split them down the middle, and laid the halves opposite each other. But he didn't split the birds. Vultures swooped down on the carcasses, but Abram scared them off. As the sun went down a deep sleep overcame Abram and then a sense of dread, dark and heavy. When the sun was down and it was dark, a smoking firepot and a flaming torch moved between the split carcasses. That's when Yah made a covenant with Abram: 'I'm giving this land to your children, from the Nile

River in Egypt to the River Euphrates in Assyria—the country of the Kenites, Kenizzites, Kadmonites, Hittites, Perizzites, Rephaim, Amorites, Canaanites, Girgashites, and Jebusites.'" (Genesis 15:9-12; 17-21)

He took Yahua at his word but as years began to pass, Sarai decides she will help the Most High give her what he has promised she and Abraham. "Now, Sarai, Abram's wife, had borne him no children. But she had an Egyptian slave named Hagar; so she said to Abram, 'The Elohim has kept me from having children. Go, sleep with my slave; perhaps I can build a family through her.' Abram agreed to what Sarai said. So after Abram had been living in Canaan ten years, Sarai his wife took her Egyptian slave Hagar and gave her to her husband to be his wife. He slept with Hagar, and she conceived." (Gen.16:1-4)

"So, Hagar bore Abram a son, and Abram gave the name Ishmael to the son she had borne." (Genesis 16:15)

When we look at human nature, we have a tendency to want to try our hand in being creator or help Yahua out in these situations. We forget He sees, and He knows the big picture. We only have an obstructed view because we only can see what has already happened not what will be. So, reciprocity takes a heap of faith also, the belief that I will get what I invested in a situation, the only catch is if the person in the situation is able to make good on their promise. Well, as we know in this case the Most High can do exceedingly above all we can hope or imagine. Here is the classic case of dealing in our own timing and desires.

While in Egypt, Abraham's wife Sarai had a handmaiden according to the custom of the time (Genesis 16:1; Ruth 16:1; Luke 1:48) and because Sarai could only understand through physical eyes, she didn't trust that the creator of the universe and of mankind could restore the function of her womb to produce life, so she gave Hagar to Abram believing she would help bring forth the seed promised to come from her husband's loins.

The custom of the time was that if a woman couldn't bear a son then the family name didn't continue. So, the custom was to use your handmaiden to give birth to your heir. The child was then raised as the offspring of the husband and wife, like a picture of today's modern surrogate mother—your expenses are paid, the seed is implanted, and you bear the child and you give it to the family to be raised and nurtured as theirs.

What Abraham's wife didn't know was that in trying to help Yahua out her husband and the handmaiden would give birth to a nation in opposition with her promised seed and the nation that Yahua promised. Some 2000 years or more later you see a picture of events set in motion. Abraham gave birth to two nations Israel and the Arab nation.

And the cycle spins out of control all because the template of truth wasn't obeyed. You may ask, "What is the template?" The template is observation of your Creator, the other created things that operate by the law of reciprocity are nature, and wildlife. These things operate and obey by the way they were commanded to function without the desire to operate by their own free will. We are the only created beings that fight against the way we were created to function.

The same is true about our lives; if we don't operate by some fundamental principles, or as I call it, live with a mission statement, we can end up with a recipe for disaster.

So many of us want respect but we have to remember to give it also. It's easy to say we want honesty, but remember, you have to be honest.

Some things in life are inevitable—good things happen to bad people and bad things happen to good people because that is the state of the world we live in; it's fallen. We don't have a choice of what family we will be born into and who we are related to, but we can choose the company we keep and the pain we allow. We can't control the choices our children will grow up and make, we can't control whether or not our spouses will cheat on us. But we can control ourselves and the pain we choose. If I want a husband, I won't choose another woman's mate and then act devastated when he does to me what he did to the last person he was with. Bad soil can't produce good fruit and unrealistic desires and urges can cause us to make bad choices that will cause us to relive old pain.

Choice sounds like such a simple word; however, it holds a lot of power. Choice has the power to unlock blessings or release curses. And choice is a gift you're given by your creator to seek Him out and choose real intimacy and fellowship with Him. He knows the best remedy for your desires. When we choose to allow our Creator to be our guide, we also receive His protection, love and providential care. After collecting unforgettable experiences and disappointments, aren't you ready to be safe in the arms of the lover of your soul? I know that I wouldn't rather be anywhere else than under the care of the one who knows me and loves me. The only string attached is to choose and obey Him.

Nowhere To Go But Up

"For if though altogether holdest thy peace at this time, then shall their enlargement and deliverance arise to Yehudah from another place; but thy fathers house shall be destroyed; and who knoweth whether though art come to the kingdom for such a time as this?"

(Esther 4:14)

In the Book of Esther, whose Hebrew name was Hadassah, she was chosen by the king who ruled in the land of her peoples captivity. There was a man by the name of Hayman who hated the Hebrews in his land, and he devised a wicked plan. This plan was to have all of the Hebrews exterminated because he claimed they had their own set of laws they lived by in the kings province. This was true. They obeyed the laws, statutes and commandments given to them by the Most High. Hayman revealed this to the king not knowing that the wife who the king's heart had grown fond of because of her grace and beauty was one of the Hebrews he wanted exterminated. Yah allowed for this young Hebrew orphan to be placed in the king's castle. By her being there at a particular time and risking her life to approach the king, she saved her nation from annihilation, and the orchestrator of the attempted genocide was hanged from his own instruments he had built for the people's execution.

Being chosen to carry the torch is a blessing and privilege just as much as it feels like a curse. Being this person requires having to build the strength and courage to persevere and push yourself past what you often thought you were incapable of. I can contest to this first hand. When I decided to write this book, I knew that there would be some adversity as well as opposition to completing the book but never in the way it has been manifested. I will be very transparent so that some of you can relate.

The desire to write has always been in my spirit because of the fact that I am very impulsive and passionate. I have found that my delivery of words is better received by others after they are written on paper and filtered by prayer. I have become aware of the fact that I can tear down with my words and encourage, writing helps me do the latter.

I also have the tendency to doubt that what I have to say will be helpful to someone else until I press pass my reservations and just do it. All my life I have been chosen to give birth to this particular book. The last 16 years of my life, I have started and stopped writing this book due to distractions, disappointments and the bold pursuance of the adversary! When I speak of distractions, they have come in the form of two bad marriages, infidelity, being a single working mother raising children, two of my five children choosing to explore and finding themselves incarcerated and now even the death of a child.

I can remember, it was three years ago that I started penning this book, and when I look at my journals from 20 years ago, I have been encountering the same opposition, so I was certain that this book was and is important and necessary. I have been given an assignment and even more so a platform to heal and change a course of direction of a whole generation of women, and hopefully men as well, to embrace who they are and what they have been through and turn their pain into purpose.

But I also can hear and feel the enemy whispering in my ear and hovering over my shoulder to frighten me from planting seeds of hope in the minds of the ones that he desires to hold captive by F.E.A.R. (false evidence appearing real). Seven years ago, as I had completely decided that no matter how frustrated I got in my marriage, no matter what my children did or didn't do, I was going to stay on the path with The Most High.

It was one night, as I was writing a lesson for my Sunday school class at the time because I hadn't quite yet come into the truth of the Sabbath. Or I thought because of tradition and indoctrination that I was doing the right thing. Long story short, I was reading Ezekiel 28 and using one of the verses for my references when I felt the presence of the enemy hovering and at the time my three-year-old was in the tub taking a bath and out of nowhere she lets out this piercing scream. I immediately run in there to see what was wrong. I asked what happened, and she shrugged her shoulders and said, "I don't know."

The adversary will oppose you at all costs when you have chosen to do a higher work. He will attack the most vulnerable and dearest ones to you. He knows that you have become aware of how he operates, and he also knows, based on observing you, what can tug at your heart strings. Isn't that something? Your enemy pays very close attention to you. "Be sober-minded; be watchful. Your adversary the devil prowls around like a roaring lion, seeking someone to devour." (1 Peter 5:8)

I got her out of the tub and prepared her for bed and then returned to my lesson to then hear this voice say, "If you write this lesson one of your children is going to die!"

My biggest fear as a mother has always been losing a child or not being there when they needed me in a time of trouble. This fear often paralyzed me or sent me into an anxiety attack because I was literally worrying about something I had no control over and hadn't happened yet.

Around this same time, my two sons would stop going to church and had begun participating in gang activity and for sure I thought this was how I would lose them and who I would lose them to. I remember fasting every Friday for my children, praying that their choices and lifestyles wouldn't consume them. The choices of others kept me so distracted and caused me to often deviate from my goal of writing. I mentioned the adversary will afflict those close to you to oppose you and cause you to stumble. So, I was also challenged with an unfaithful husband and numerous women that had made themselves available for his selfish desires. Some unaware and some willing to participate. These distractions would come in the form of an angry side piece revealing his indiscretions and theirs while trying to play the victim while committing adultery and be mad because they found out they weren't the only side piece to his meal. This behavior kept me pretty frustrated and distracted. Meanwhile, tradition and bad theology kept me trying to salvage the broken covenant of a marriage. In all of the situations mentioned, I was doing all of the work. Most of the work was maintaining my sanity and not allowing others' behaviors and decisions to kill my character.

Two years later, my 19-year-old son would get sentenced to five and one half years in prison, and my youngest son would become incarcerated as well. All of this while the person who was supposed to be protecting and covering was leaving me open to attacks from all areas. So, my main focus remained trying to stay sane and submit to the headship of Yah. I was still trying to be all things to everyone by supporting my troubled sons, all the while putting my divinely ordered assignment and desires on the back burner. As I mentioned previously, my earnest desire is to change the course of direction for someone on the same road or contemplating the fact that they are stuck in a rut, and to please the Creator by bringing honor to His name.

The final blow was in November 2017 when my worst nightmare came true; my beautiful twenty-six-year-old daughter and newborn granddaughter transcended from time to eternity. Trying to explain this feeling is like trying to explain childbirth to a barren woman. After sleeping at a hospital for seven days praying, fasting and hoping for the best, I was left a completely different person. I was leaving the hospital missing a person that I had spent 26 years nurturing and loving, this is when I realized something, nothing but me dying myself was going to kill me and regardless of whatever is going on around me, the enemy can only distract and make noise and nothing can hurt more than this. Most parents don't get the assignment of having to bury both their child and their grandchild at the same time! I am convinced something marvelous has to be birthed out of this. This much pain has convinced me to complete all missions placed before me. Prayerfully, I am determined to walk out what I have been entrusted to do.

I am a child that was raised by at least one parent with a narcissistic personality disorder. I am convinced that the personality is the malignant type, but I am not a therapist. This type of nurturing caused me, in the attempt to never be like this person, to end up in relationships with people with the same personality type and be subjected to the same guilt, ridicule and neediness. All the while they try and mask the neediness in the form of control and often abuse. May it be verbal, emotional or physical. It has taken years to create strong boundaries and the affects may take longer to recover from. Although you may not have had the same experiences I have wrestled, your experience is yours and are valid to you and you may be able to relate.

Pain can seem like the only emotion that has been consistent. No matter how loving, caring and fair you know how to be, the return for your sincerity always seems to be pain and adversity coupled with betrayal and disappointment. Lately, some of the most genuine women that I have come in contact with all express the same experience, and that experience is brokenness; and they are struggling for answers. This seems prevalent in some of the most resilient people I know. People are tired of the old cliché statements. We need people who will be transparent and share what they are going through or what they have made it through, so that the one caught in the storm can see their way out and know that there is life on the other side of pain.

It was revealed to me through a lot of soul searching and struggling to forgive repeat offenders that I have endured adversity to break generational curses. There has been an urgency placed on my heart to break the cycle of brokenness when I realized that the same people that kept offending were on nonstop rollercoasters and didn't know how to push the stop button or where to look for help. I realized that habitually making bad choices was what held them hostage and resulted in them experiencing a lower quality of life. I may not be able to stop my repeat offenders, but I could be the change I wanted to see.

From the moment we are shaped and formed in our mother's womb, we were developing with the purpose and intentionality. Our Creator chose the parents we would come forth through to exist and our parents' choices determined the environment we would be raised and nurtured in. As you can see, all of these things were picked for us before we even had the ability to reason. We had no choice in the family that we would be born into and all of these factors were the beginning and the most important part of who you would become. You are born with your father's DNA, but you inherit your mother's soul or character, and this was by far no accident.

My birth order and the family I had been born into, and not to mention the series of events that transpired in my young life and teenage years, revealed to me that I was born to carry the torch. No one endures this much pain and adversity and still has the ability to love, reason and move on. "There must be a reason for all of this," I often would rehearse in my thoughts.

My path was one that consisted of secrets, lies and a quest to embrace this roar I always felt fighting to emerge from the pit of my soul, but there was always a force trying to mute the passion within me. Whether it was by a parent who didn't understand how to nurture a child with the personality I possessed or the whispering from the enemy reminding me that I was less than because of the things that I was subjected to endure. I have lived with a guardian who lacked the ability to protect anyone's interest but their own. So, I learned to protect and advocate for myself. I have decided to quit waiting for others to tell me who I am and believe the truth about what Yah says about me. He says that I am beloved and chosen and I am his: "I have called you by name, you are mine" (Isaiah 43:1) My very name means purpose, so I know this was no coincidence. I am determined to see myself the way Yah sees me. I have had the tendency to see myself the way others who didn't deserve me treated me. Subscribing to the thoughts Yah has for me changed my course of direction.

"For I know the thoughts that I think toward you, saith the LORD, thoughts of peace, and not of evil, to give you an expected end." (Jeremiah 29:11)

This gave me a desire to seek and search for the presence that I felt resided in and around me. Some of those quests weren't in the manuscript so I would go back to get a better understanding as to why was I here. I wanted to do more, and I always wanted to go deeper and get to the root of how people ended up at certain pit stops in life. I never realized that the deeper you go and the more you understand, the bigger the burden to change what is revealed to you will become.

"Call to me and I will answer you and tell you great and incomprehensible things you do not know." (Jeremiah 33:3)

I saw others that had been chosen to change generational curses and break toxic family cycles and always wondered what caused them to drop the ball.

As I would question others poor choices of behavior and life patterns as a youth, my aunt Bertha would gently rebuke me and say, "Just keep living, baby, just keep living." This quote, to me now, says more than she could ever elaborate on. Life is a journey and you have to take the good with the bad and keep moving. Sometimes you will have to leave some things and people behind to elevate. There will sometimes be some hard questions you will have to ask yourself and then tell yourself the truth in the answer?

Do I blend in like everybody else or do I change the things that I see and don't like? Am I willing to invest in helping people? Helping others requires giving components and resources from yourself. Am I willing to invest? If you are one that desires to see healing come from obscure situations, beware not to get sucked in and consumed by the people you desire to help.

People in toxic patterns are often comfortable there. This is all they know, and to break cycles means some painful things have to be dealt with and uncovered. *Breaking cycles is like removing cancer if you don't treat it, it continues to spread.*

When you have been blessed to come out of adversity, I believe it is your responsibility to change the things that were designed to break you and didn't.

"I beseech you therefore, brethren, by the mercies of Yah, that ye present your bodies a living sacrifice, holy, acceptable unto Yah, *which is* your reasonable service." (Romans12:1)

When you have overcome obstacles, you should not let the next generation coming up recycle the same pain you have been served up. Others have lived so wounded for so long that they think it's ok.

These are the people whose hands you hold until they can stand on their own truth. Fighting to change a wounded heart will be met with opposition and resistance. But remember the reason for all of the adversity you have endured. The adversity was training and tempering you to lead. Be the person to someone that you always desired.

"Don't let your good be evil spoken of." (Romans 14:16)

Being passionate, coupled with a caring and loving heart can be misconstrued sometimes or may I state, "most of the time." If you generally have a love for people, they will question your intentions or think you have ulterior motives. Don't let this change your focus. The worst thing about caring and being a person who wants to see change is that you end up being misunderstood or you see more potential in people than they see in themselves. Some people will have to be left behind, but if you stay the course, you will see miraculous things transpire when you have the courage to make a ripple in the pond.

One of the most frustrating things that will happen when you are making progress is the distractions that will come; they manifest by way of being lied on and misunderstood by people who won't take the time to know what drives you and there will be others who want you to do all the healing work for them.. Stay the course, what you're doing will work.

Then there will be people that you least expect to meet you on your journey. Those will be the ones who Yah has placed in your path for this journey. They have gone before you and are divinely set in your path to walk with you. To my surprise, they were never the people that I thought they would be. I have just recently experienced this truth. The ones I least expect came along side of me at one of my darkest and hardest times in my life. During the concluding of this book, my 26-year-old daughter who was nine months pregnant, had a severe asthma attack and had an emergency cesarean section. For seven days, she and her newborn daughter were on life support. She passed away from the effects of the attack on the 7th day and my granddaughter, which was her 4th child, went to be with her mother in paradise three days later. My world felt like it collapsed and I, at this time, asked the Creator, "Who do you think I am? I can't do this." The thought of losing any of my children was something I never wanted to imagine, but now being faced with losing my daughter and her daughter was paralyzing. I asked Yah "Why do you think I can handle this?" And in my praying and meditating on a response from Yah I was met with, "What I am going to do in this situation will sit well with you." I thought that this answer meant she would make a full recovery, but my baby transitioned, and her soul was promoted. Baby Rhikki followed soon after, and when I prayed and meditated after her passing, I was met with a response that reminded me that, "Yah does all things well" (Mark 7:37). So, during the planning of her service I had the song "It is well with my soul" (Horatio Spafford) sang at her funeral as to say amen to with the lot that had been dealt to me as a mother. I also am grasping the concept of being born for adversity and such a time as this. What we go through is never about us, especially when you have surrendered your life to the Master. You are His, and He uses all that He equipped you with as a beacon and a light to draw others to him. Needless to say, as many believe and have said that 26 was far too young to leave her husband a widower and three other children without their mom. Her life was extremely full. I often remember reminding her that she had a huge influence on young women her age; she was beautiful, outspoken, artistic, funny and loyal. She was a hairstylist at the pinnacle of her craft and a dedicated wife, mother, sister and friend. The impact of her loss captured the whole community's attention, young and old. In my grief, I often would say all of the things I had planned and invested in my baby was for her to carry the torch in the beauty industry. I was ready to move in another direction and do other things that I wanted to accomplish like open a cosmetology school and teach all aspects of beauty. I really almost gave in to depression. Then healing caused me to realized that my vessel had to be broken for the best of the contents to be poured out. My daughter and granddaughter are my seeds from brokenness that will promote more growth.

Be encouraged, investing in others will reveal that everyone you invest in isn't going to love you especially, when your truth sheds light on things they don't have the courage to deal with. Second, you will experience people that pretend to like you so that they can stay close enough to receive the benefits of being in your presence. Know when to exit.

Last but not least, even if a person doesn't like you, they will respect you for not wavering about what you stand for.

Remember to live intentionally; make sure your talk lines up with your walk, whether you want to be a mentor or not, someone is always looking for a leader. Remember that to err is human but to not learn from the experience is when you should be embarrassed. The people that I have learned to respect and admire are those who assume responsibility for their actions; no blaming or pointing fingers but correcting and making their wrongs right, as soon as possible.

"For a righteous *man* may fall seven times. And rise again, but the wicked shall fall by calamity." (Proverbs 24:16)

Everybody can't handle the truth, and this chapter is written for the ones that can.

Everyone won't admit it, but most are looking for someone to lead them to truth and out of a dark situation. Little do you know that person is you.

When you feel like quitting, remind yourself that renovating is messy and some of the people that you will encounter are hurting and have been hurt by people that they only wanted love from.

Passionate and powerful people will always be seen as a source of strength for others that aren't fully equipped to withstand the storms of life and they will seek you to be their refuge. The goal is to hold their hand until they are able to walk. Make sure that before you pour out that you have tapped into the right energy source. For me personally, Yah has been the one who fills me when I am empty.

Beware of joy robbers and askholes! The joy robbers are the ones who always have a problem but never want a solution. They just love pep talks so that when you offer a solution, they have a reason why they cannot use the solution to cure their problem… they love their situation.

"Speak not in the ears of a fool: for he will despise the wisdom of thy words." (Proverbs 23:9)

Leave them where they are. Some askholes just want a motivational speaker and want to hear what is on your mind so that they can share your situation if you have exposed it. Remember that after you have spoken truth in love and shown compassion and are rejected, dust off your sandals and move on, someone is really starving for truth, quit wasting it on the people that only like to analyze problems but won't do a thing to change them.

Psalms 119:43-47 says: "For I trust in the word and do not take the word of truth utterly out of my mouth far wait For the ordinances. So I will keep thy law continually for ever and ever. And I will walk at liberty and I seek thy precepts. I will also speak of the testimony before kings and shall not be ashamed. And I will delight myself in thy commandments, which I have love: and I will meditate in thy statutes."

Having power and a testimony is not accomplished without adversity, your challenges and failures are a setup for The Most High to put you on display and a light to guide others out of their darkness.

As I survey the record, persevering through adversity produces some amazing people. Let's take a look at Moses, he was born to Hebrew slaves and saved from the pharaoh's wrath of killing baby boys to eventually wind up being raised, educated and trained for war in the pharaoh's house. He answered the call later to lead Israel out of bondage. Moses denounced the privileges and status of being in pharaoh's home and chose to be the advocate for his people. This would result in Moses killing an Egyptian and running to hide for 40 years in Midian. Yah met him in the wilderness and spoke to him at a burning bush. Yah gave Moses a commission and he answered the call to lead Israel, the chosen people of Yah, to the promised land. Moses participated in establishing Yah's nation from people who had been oppressed and suffered great loss. Moses was born at a time when the pharaoh was killing all of the male Hebrew babies. His mother made a huge leap of faith and fashioned a basket that would withstand the water of the Nile. This basket would find its way to the pharaoh's daughter who would raise this child as her own. This mother trusted that Yah does all things well also. This was no easy task if you read the story in Exodus chapters 4-12 you will see this task seemed impossible. Because of his belief and perseverance, Moses was used for great tasks by Yah.

Let's take a look at Esther, orphaned at an early age and raised buy her uncle, she wound up in the king's palace and her obedience and sacrifice saved the Hebrew nation from genocide.

Last but not least, the most important example we have is Yahshua; he was born to die. "Who hath believed our report and to whom is the arm of the Lord revealed? For he shall grow up before him as a tender plant, and as a root out of a dry ground: he hath no form nor comeliness; and when we shall see him, there is no beauty that we should desire him. He is despised and rejected of men; a man of sorrows, and acquainted with grief: and we hid as it were our faces from him; he was despised, and we esteemed him not. Surely he hath borne our griefs, and carried our sorrows: yet we did esteem him stricken, smitten of God, and afflicted. But he was wounded for our transgressions, he was bruised for our iniquities: the chastisement of our peace was upon him; and with his stripes we are healed. All we like sheep have gone astray; we have turned everyone to his own way; and the Lord hath laid on him the iniquity of us all. He was oppressed, and he was afflicted, yet he opened not his mouth: he is brought as a lamb to the slaughter, and as a sheep before her shearers is dumb, so he openeth not his mouth. He was taken from prison and from judgment: and who shall declare his generation? for he was cut off out of the land of the living: for the transgression of my people was he stricken. And he made his grave with the wicked, and with the rich in his death; because he had done no violence, neither was any deceit in his mouth. Yet it pleased Yahua to bruise him; he hath put him to grief: when thou shalt make his soul an offering for sin, he shall see his seed, he shall prolong his days, and the pleasure of Yahua shall prosper in his hand. He shall see of the travail of his soul, and shall be satisfied: by his knowledge shall my righteous servant justify many; for he shall bear their iniquities. Therefore will I divide him a portion with the great, and he shall divide the spoil with the strong; because he hath poured out his soul unto death: and he was numbered with the transgressors; and he bare the sin of many, and made intercession for the transgressors." (Isaiah 53:1-12)

Born to break the power of sin and its mastery over our lives.

So much pain exists in our communities and families because most of the ancient markers have been removed, curses have perpetuated because the elders have left their post. We have learned the ways of nations that have oppressed us and forgot how instrumental our culture and history is, and how it has shaped most of modern civilization.

A lot of us have taken the bait and believe that new is better.

"What has been will be again, what has been done will be done again; there is nothing new under the sun." (Ecclesiastes 1:9)

We have failed to trust the one that existed from antiquity. "But now thus saith ELOHIM that created you, O Jacob, and he that formed you, O Israel, Fear not: for I have redeemed you, I have called you by your name; you are mine. When you pass through the waters, I will be with you; and through the rivers, they shall not overflow you: when you walk through the fire, you shall not be burned; neither shall the flame kindle on you. For I am Yahuah your Elohim, the Holy One of Israel, your Savior: I gave Egypt for your ransom, Ethiopia and Seba for you. Since you were precious in my sight, you have been honorable, and I have loved you: therefore will I give men for you, and people for your life. Fear not: for I am with you: I will bring your seed from the east, and gather you from the west; I will say to the north, Give up; and to the south, Keep not back: bring my sons from far, and my daughters from the ends of the earth; Even every one that is called by my name: for I have created him for my glory, I have formed him; yes, I have made him. Bring forth the blind people that have eyes, and the deaf that have ears. Let all the nations be gathered together, and let the people be assembled: who among them can declare this, and show us former things? let them bring forth their witnesses, that they may be justified: or let them hear, and say, It is truth. You are my witnesses, saith Yahua, and my servant whom I have chosen: that you may know and believe me, and understand that I am he: before me there was no Elohim formed, neither shall there be after me. I, even I, am Yahua; and beside me there is no savior. I have declared, and have saved, and I have showed, when there was no strange god among you: therefore you are my witnesses, said the Yahua, that I am Elohim. Yes, before the day was I am he; and there is none that can deliver out of my hand: I will work, and who shall let it?" (Isaiah 43:1-12)

We have to realize that we are fighting for our inheritance, fighting for our bloodline and future. When we don't have knowledge of who we are and from what tree we've come from, we don't realize how important we are. The future offspring and the generations after us deserve to know that cycles can be broken. We have learned to live under the curses so long that we have the mentality of every man for himself, but it couldn't be further from the way Yah designed community and family to operate. Someone has to guide and cultivate and teach. It is up to those that have been chosen and have overcome challenges to cultivate the soil of the coming generations. We must produce new life and restore value and worth in people; you must be willing to plant good seed from the new fruit that was put in your life.

Some people will be divinely sent, and some will be sent by the adversary, remain prayerful and watching and most of all listen to their speech. The enemy knows the word too, make sure you know it in the right context. "For He shall give His angels charge over you, To keep you in all your ways. In *their* hands they shall bear you up, Lest you dash your foot against a stone." (Psalms 91:11-12)

Then Yeshua was led up by the Spirit into the wilderness to be tempted by the devil. And when He had fasted forty days and forty nights, afterward He was hungry. Now when the tempter came to Him, he said, "If You are the Son of Yahua, command that these stones become bread." But He answered and said, "It is written, 'Man shall not live by bread alone, but by every word that proceeds from the mouth of Yahua.'" Then the devil took Him up into the holy city, set Him on the pinnacle of the temple, and said to Him, "If You are the Son of Yahua, throw Yourself down. For it is written:

'He shall give His angels charge over you,' and, 'In *their* hands they shall bear you up, Lest you dash your foot against a stone.'" Yeshua said to him, "It is written again, 'You shall not tempt the Yahua your Elohim.'" Again, the devil took Him up on an exceedingly high mountain and showed Him all the kingdoms of the world and their glory. And he said to Him, "All these things I will give You if You will fall down and worship me." Then Yeshua said to him, "Away with you, Satan! For it is written, 'You shall worship the Yahua your Elohim, and Him only you shall serve.'" Then the devil left Him, and behold, angels came and ministered to Him. (Matt. 4:1-11)

He will mix the truth with a lie and have you spiraling out of control and you will end up helping the wrong team: "Now the serpent was more crafty than any of the wild animals the Yahua Elohim had made. He said to the woman, "Did Yahua really say, 'You must not eat from any tree in the garden'?"

The woman said to the serpent, "We may eat fruit from the trees in the garden, but Yahua did say, 'You must not eat fruit from the tree that is in the middle of the garden, and you must not touch it, or you will die.'"

"You will not certainly die," the serpent said to the woman. "For Yahua knows that when you eat from it your eyes will be opened, and you will be like Yahua , knowing good and evil."

When the woman saw that the fruit of the tree was good for food and pleasing to the eye, and also desirable for gaining wisdom, she took some and ate it. She also gave some to her husband, who was with her, and he ate it. Then the eyes of both of them were opened, and they realized they were naked; so they sewed fig leaves together and made coverings for themselves.

Then the man and his wife heard the sound of the Yahua Elohim as he was walking in the garden in the cool of the day, and they hid from Yahua Elohim among the trees of the garden. But the Yahua Elohim called to the man, "Where are you?"

He answered, "I heard you in the garden, and I was afraid because I was naked; so I hid."

And he said, "Who told you that you were naked? Have you eaten from the tree that I commanded you not to eat from?"

The man said, "The woman you put here with me—she gave me some fruit from the tree, and I ate it."

Then the Yahua Elohim said to the woman, "What is this you have done?"

The woman said, "The serpent deceived me, and I ate."

So the Yahua Elohim said to the serpent, "Because you have done this, Cursed are you above all livestock and all wild animals! You will crawl on your belly and you will eat dust all the days of your life. And I will put enmity between you and the woman, and between your offspring and hers; he will crush your head, and you will strike his heel."

To the woman he said, "I will make your pains in childbearing very severe; with painful labor you will give birth to children. Your desire will be for your husband, and he will rule over you."

To Adam he said, "Because you listened to your wife and ate fruit from the tree about which I commanded you, 'You must not eat from it.'"

"Cursed is the ground because of you; through painful toil you will eat food from it all the days of your life. It will produce thorns and thistles for you, and you will eat the plants of the field. By the sweat of your brow you will eat your food until you return to the ground since from it you were taken; for dust you are and to dust you will return." Adam named his wife Eve, because she would become the mother of all the living. Yahua Elohim made garments of skin for Adam and his wife and clothed them. And Yahua Elohim said, "The man has now become like one of us, knowing good and evil. He must not be allowed to reach out his hand and take also from the tree of life and eat, and live forever." So, the Yahua Elohim banished him from the Garden of Eden to work the ground from which he had been taken. After he drove the man out, he placed on the east side of the Garden of Eden cherubim and a flaming sword flashing back and forth to guard the way to the tree of life." (Gen. 3:1-24)

Every generation has a chance to break curses because we all have a purpose, what will be the mark that you leave in the universe?

It was said of the prophet David that after he completed his task for his generation he slept with elders. "Now when David had served Yah's purpose in his own generation, he fell asleep; he was buried with his ancestors and his body decayed." (Acts.13:36) Our bodies will die and decay but your word, deeds and the influence you had in the physical realm will continue.

We are surrounded by a great cloud of witnesses; others are looking for someone to show them how they can make it over so don't forfeit it. "Therefore, since we are surrounded by such a great cloud of witnesses, let us throw off everything that hinders and the sin that so easily entangles. And let us run with perseverance the race marked out for us, fixing our eyes on Yeshua, the pioneer and perfecter of faith. For the joy set before him he endured the cross, scorning its shame, and sat down at the right hand of the throne of Yah. Consider him who endured such opposition from sinners, so that you will not grow weary and lose heart." (Hebrews 12)

Don't watch another walk in your destiny because you delayed fulfilling your purpose when the torch was passed to you.

How many of us are serving our purpose in our generation? Why are so many of us merely just existing? What good will we do for our generation when we transcend but don't leave a mark for the next generation to follow? Some of us will leave curses because we chose to let adversity and pain master us instead of using the stumbling blocks placed in our paths as stepping stones.

We exist in the time now where our markers to the way of life that worked have been removed, leaving so many of us lacking a point of reference to model after. Due to the lack of direction, most people leave this universe and have not left words or instructions for the next generation to follow and have prosperity.

"A good *man* leaves an inheritance to his children's children, but the wealth of the sinner is stored up for the righteous." (Proverbs 13:22)

Be the one that does, you finish a long journey one step at a time, start restoring what has been damaged so that those coming up behind you will have shelter from some of life's storms and not be left with questions that have not been answered by others who chose to suppress truth.

Share your triumphs and failures with those observing your life, because we learn by observation and then walking it out. With life, sometimes the test comes first and then the theory of why we are starts to make sense. Again, don't leave those that are seeking truth in the dark. No one can identify with a person who isn't willing to be transparent, and who portrays to have never failed at life. There is much respect given when you can share what has oppressed you and that which has empowered you. It's encouraging to know someone who has overcome when it looked like all the odds were against them. No matter what some people will feel like, their choices will bring a completely different outcome because that's just human nature. Don't be angry with them, just remain neutral and loving, so that when they return broken you can speak life back into them and encourage them.

One thing I know about life is you can't cheat the grid; most people will be truthful and tell you if you try to cheat the grid you have to back track to where you started cheating at it and do it right. Life doesn't grade on a curve, but it gives you back what you invest .

We are all actors in the bigger script called preparing for eternity and you only get one shot. The script has been written once and for all, and revisions aren't an option when it comes to being obedient to your call and position in life; however, the crowns are given to all who endure, obey, trust and love the script writer.

Your willingness, passion and pain will sanctify and securely guide the one coming up in the next generation who is willing to embrace it.

No great work goes unnoticed, it may go unnoticed by the one you want to see it but believe me, it is blessing someone else and they are gaining velocity by watching and seeing that they are capable because of what they see you share about overcoming.

The best news is that your pain can become your triumph; it is apparent that we live in a fallen world and pain is something we'll all experience, but when you embrace your position and know your identity and that others just like you have persevered and made it, you can rest assured that the Creator's heart's desire is for you to surrender and trust him. "Cease *striving* and know that I am Yah; I will be exalted among the nations, I will be exalted in the earth." (Psalms 46:10)

Eve became the first mother of a martyr because of disobedience, but she became the mother of all living through obedience. Sarah being a barren women past the age of childbirth had faith in Yah and his promise. Even when situations seemed humanly impossible, she bore a son who was promised to her by her creator. (Gen. 21:2) Deborah became the judge of Israel, giving counsel and wisdom (Judges 4-5) and although Ruth was a pagan and a foreigner, her faith captured the heart of King Boaz. (Book of Ruth)

Rahab was a harlot, but for fear in Yahua, she saved her entire family and her faith landed her in the lineage of our Savior. (Joshua 2), (Matt 1:5) Hannah was ridiculed for not being able to bear a child but became the portrait of grace and gave birth to a prophet. (1 Sam.) Although Anna was a widow, her faithfulness and service in the temple allowed her to see her Savior before she died. (Luke 2:25-35) Mary was the topic of many rumors and the topic of hurtful discussions, but because she believed in the one who could not lie, she became the mother of the one who would give salvation to the world. (Luke 1:26-45)

The call to elevate is one that few accept. Many have been chosen but few have accepted, many tables have been prepared to accomplish the will and plans of Yah. You have to take your rightful seat and be the change you desire to see.

All Storms Aren't Punishment

"Purge me with hyssop, and I shall be clean: wash me, and I shall be whiter than snow."

(Psalms 51:7)

I know we have all heard the term *a recipe for disaster*. Or the theory of Murphy's Law: whatever can go wrong will go wrong. How about the perfect storm where all the stars align, and all components jive together to create the paradigm shift of a lifetime?

Some people's lives literally look like they were born to manifest this theory. We've seen the principle, which I have touched on more often than I would like to admit. My favorite aunt often says: "If you don't deal with the truth about how you arrived somewhere, you'll become a repeat offender of the situation and you can slip into deep, deep darkness and not even know it."

All storms aren't punishment and don't come to break you but to set you up to develop you into the masterpiece you were designed to be.

I will use the concept of gardening and picture to convey this principle. If you are a student of the Bible, you will notice that most of Yeshua's teachings related to the bio agricultural community and culture they lived in. He dealt with reaping and sowing as well as cycles of growth to facilitate others in getting what he spoke about. Being taught scripture from a western mindset (abstract) which involves rationalism and individual understanding through rational deductive thought and segregated thinking. So, most of us have not been able to understand some of the parables that Yeshua taught based on rational deductive thought. Yeshua dealt in concrete terms the way the Hebraic minds understood how the parables appealed to our five senses. We could see it, taste, touch, smell, and hear it. Scripture, as life is, was meant to be observable. And sometimes it can look like life is getting the upper hand. It can appear that before we fully materialize, we undergo what looks like to those on the outside peering in that we are dying. Or that life will totally consume us. In planting, seeds go into the ground and reproduce after their own kind. An amazing series of events takes place before the fruit is visible. Before I began to study Hebrew, I didn't think about the fact that the entire life was contained in the seed, but as long as the seed remains in the package it will never produce anything. It is only when the seed is placed in soil and covered that the components that are contained in the seed are activated.

My oldest daughter home schools my two granddaughters. They have been on the life cycle of plants and one of the projects she and the girls recently did involved placing soil in individual planters and then adding seeds into individual planters with covered tops. This allows the seed to develop its roots in nutrient rich soil. This process is called germination. Once the root takes hold then a small plant emerges and breaks through the soil. This is the most exciting part after weeks of watching to see what will happen to the seed that was carefully placed in the soil. Some seeds don't turn into plants and others do. Some don't develop strong enough roots, so once removed from the starter planters they can't withstand the outside elements and perish. But the plants that thrive go on to produce fruits and vegetables with more seeds that can be planted.

This classroom project blessed me and gave me a more vivid analogy of how carefully my/our creator cares for us. You may ask how is plant life equivocal to human life? And I will say, "All things created have a cycle and testify of our Creator and his love." For example, just by looking at a seed with the human eye you only see a seed. But contained inside the seed is the ability to produce a crop that gives life. You may be able to identify a bean, pumpkin seed, or watermelon seed. However, whether or not the seed possesses the components to go through the planting process and produce fruit can only be determined once it is placed in the soil. The planting process is determined by the gardener. The gardener makes sure the soil is fertile either by testing its composition or by purchasing the soil from a reputable nursery. Then the gardener waits until it is the right season for the seed to be planted. All of this is essential to getting the best results. There are some crops that withstand all four seasons. Then summer crop, fall crop, winter crop and spring crop and they can only be placed outside then. Unless they are grown in a controlled environment like a greenhouse.

With technology, gardening and growing has become so sophisticated you can now grow using hydroponics; which is growing plants without soil by only using mineral nutrient solutions in a water solvent. Aeroponics: instead of putting plants in water the plants are misted with nutrient rich water. Aquaponics: is a combination of hydroponics and aquaculture, therefore producing both food and organic produce. The fish waste is upcycled as the plants can use the fish waste for nutrients. The plants grow faster, and less water is used. I gave all of these examples of growth to state the fact that the gardener is the one who chooses the environment to produce where the life of the plant will be sustained.

Such it is with us; we all appear, to the visible eye, to be human. We may be from different regions, nations, and tribes. We may speak different languages and may have different or similar beliefs, but one thing remains true… "The creator of the universe chose where we would have our beginning. And he made from one man every nation of mankind to live on all the face of the earth, having determined allotted periods and the boundaries of their dwelling place, that they should seek God, and perhaps feel their way toward him and find him. Yet he is actually not far from each one of us." (Acts 17:26-27)

We are all spiritual beings having a human experience. We are traveling through space and time having been planted as a seed in the nutrient rich womb of our mothers. When the time was right, we emerged from her matrix and were placed in a family. In this family you were nurtured, trained and hopefully loved until you were able to sustain life for yourself. The capacity we possess to show the evidence of what we are made of can only be revealed when we are planted.

Some of us have endured so many storms, it seems like we would never get to our destination; this is just the development process. Platforms were created for masterpieces and you don't display your masterpiece until it is perfect, and the timing is just right. When I observed my storms through the lens of a gardener, I see the purpose protected spaces and then being placed in what seems like dark isolated spaces at times. He sees us and is carefully watching us, especially when he knows the components that we possess and what we will become if we weather the storms of life. I recently had a conversation with my sister, and she was going through why she didn't have any expectations out of Yah answering personal prayers. In this conversation, she expressed the fact that he may answer a nation's prayers once they are praying on one accord and acting in obedience. This opinion was being expressed by her because she has been experiencing the storms of life and questions Yah's will for her life, individually.

"Blessed is the one who does not walk in step with the wicked or stand in the way that sinners take or sit in the company of mockers, but whose delight is in the law of Yahua, and who meditates on his law day and night. That person is like a tree planted by streams of water, which yields its fruit in season and whose leaf does not wither—whatever they do prospers. Not so the wicked! They are like chaff that the wind blows away. Therefore the wicked will not stand in the judgment, nor sinners in the assembly of the righteous. For Yahua watches over the way of the righteous, but the way of the wicked leads to destruction." (Psalms 1:1-6)

So, being a giver, or one who loves deeply, I have often been met with lots of adversity. I've always been a cheerleader for the underdog. I love to see the one that others have canceled out win. The more I examine life and the people that have been strategically placed in my circles, I realize some were placed there because I invited them, thinking that I can be of some assistance in their growth. Only later to find out that they were being used as the character in the chapter in my book called, "Lessons Learned in the Storm," to tell how they challenged me to grow.

I've learned that all pain is not punishment, because Yah is in control of the entire universe and its creation. He has all power. I often hear people saying the devil is busy, true but they need to realize, yeah, he is only busy with the things

he's allowed to do. He has to get permission from his creator who is Yah to attack you or even touch your life.

"There was a man in the land of Uz, whose name was Job; and that man was perfect and upright, and one that feared Yahua, and eschewed evil. And there were born unto him seven sons and three daughters. His substance also was seven thousand sheep, and three thousand camels, and five hundred yoke of oxen, and five hundred she asses, and a very great household; so that this man was the greatest of all the men of the east. And his sons went and feasted in their houses, every one his day; and sent and called for their three sisters to eat and to drink with them. And it was so, when the days of their feasting were gone about, that Job sent and sanctified them, and rose up early in the morning, and offered burnt offerings according to the number of them all: for Job said, It may be that my sons have sinned, and cursed Yahua in their hearts. Thus did Job continually. Now there was a day when the sons of Yahua came to present themselves before the Lord, and Satan came also among them. And Yahua said unto Satan, Whence comest thou? Then Satan answered Yahua, and said, From going to and fro in the earth, and from walking up and down in it. And Yahua said unto Satan, Hast thou considered my servant Job, that there is none like him in the earth, a perfect and an upright man, one that feareth Yahua, and escheweth evil? Then Satan answered Yahua, and said, Doth Job fear Yahua for nought? Hast not thou made an hedge about him, and about his house, and about all that he hath on every side? thou hast blessed the work of his hands, and his substance is increased in the land. But put forth thine hand now, and touch all that he hath, and he will curse thee to thy face. And Yahua said unto Satan, Behold, all that he hath is in thy power; only upon himself put not forth thine hand. So Satan went forth from the presence of Yahua. And there was a day when his sons and his daughters were eating and drinking wine in their eldest brother's house: And there came a messenger unto Job, and said, The oxen were plowing, and the asses feeding beside them: And the Sabeans fell upon them, and took them away; yea, they have slain the servants with the edge of the sword; and I only am escaped alone to tell thee. While he was yet speaking, there came also another, and said, The fire of Yahua is fallen from heaven, and hath burned up the sheep, and the servants, and consumed them; and I only am escaped alone to tell thee. While he was yet speaking, there came also another, and said, The Chaldeans made out three bands, and fell upon the camels, and have carried them away, yea, and slain the servants with the edge of the sword;

and I only am escaped alone to tell thee. While he was yet speaking, there came also another, and said, Thy sons and thy daughters were eating and drinking wine in their eldest brother's house: And, behold, there came a great wind from the wilderness, and smote the four corners of the house, and it fell upon the young men, and they are dead; and I only am escaped alone to tell thee. Then Job arose, and rent his mantle, and shaved his head, and fell down upon the ground, and worshipped, And said, Naked came I out of my mother's womb, and naked shall I return thither: Yahua gave, and Yahua hath taken away; blessed be the name of Yahua. In all this Job sinned not, nor charged Elohim foolishly." (Job 1:3 11 -27)

Remember in your storms that Yah has put every tool you will need for the storm in you or others that he will send to cover you while you go through. "A friend loves at all times, and a brother is born for a time of adversity." (Proverbs 17:17)

The storm isn't sent to destroy you, but it was allowed to make you more dependent on Him. Just like revelation of truth is progressive, so is a storm and its strength but only to build character in those that love and obey Him.

1 Cor. 10:13 says: "No temptation has overtaken you but such as is common to man and Yah is faithful, who will not allow you to be tempted beyond what you are able, but with the temptation will provide the way of escape also that you may be able to endure it."

This is fantastic news, I am happy just being able to convey this truth to you! I have literally survived the same adversity that I believed with all of my heart would destroy me.

Most storm riders I know were always being prepared for a platform, they just didn't know it. The Creator I know always does everything with excellence and in His timing. Just as an artist knows that presentation is everything, He knows when you have come through the storm you will be ready to be on display for His glory.

I have a childhood friend who didn't learn to cook until later in life. She has many other great qualities but loving the kitchen was never one of them. Unlike myself, I love to cook and get creative with my dishes and the presentation of them. One night, my girl was on Snapchat cooking up a meal and I was like, ok check her out! What she was cooking looked good as it was being prepared. The moment arrived for her to display what she had so proudly labored over and that is when I gasped!

Was she presenting her meal on a paper plate? My jaw dropped! I immediately texted her and said, "Girlfriend, presentation is everything! You don't showcase your masterpiece on a paper plate!" It became a laughable moment but there was so much truth in this experience.

My advice to a friend was an epiphany to me as well. Immediately, Yah spoke to my heart and said, "Daughter, you're absolutely right. I don't present my handiwork on paper plates either. The fire that you are being tried by now is just a prelude to the masterpiece I'm creating you to become, keep pressing forward." I have realized that we identify the things in other people that we have really going on in our hearts. If it wasn't true how could you identify it in another's life?

So, I'll give you a full disclosure moment: I would often speak to myself and say; "There has to be more to life than this." This walk with the Lord has to be more than this. I mean, I know life is more than waking up grinding all day at work and just paying bills, just to get up and do it all over again. More than having one bad relationship after another and raising children to wait to live and then die tired and unfulfilled. I have seen more real-life horror stories than I care to elaborate on and if it is the last thing I do, "I will experience the joy of life." I would say. I can remember praying, serving on church ministries, teaching the ladies groups and planning women's retreats only to still feel like there is more to the big picture than this!

I would often wonder why my process to give birth to my dreams was taking so long, all I wanted was to see my desires come to fruition. All along, Yah was waiting for me to line up with Him and obey. Obedience to Yah's commandments was the key to unlocking the things that had been placed in my heart. I realized I had a zeal but not according to knowledge. I was being disobedient, in all that I was doing I was following the template of tradition and theologians. I was creating enmity and not walking in his will. I was executing my own will and choices for my life and praying amiss to a creator whose word doesn't change. He knows the thoughts he has toward me and my expected end. I don't know what's best for me, he does. And before things can line up perfectly with the will Yah has for your life, some things have to be turned upside down. It wasn't until I began to really follow Him the way he requires that he began to place the right resources in my path. He has allowed more than what I hoped for to take place in my life.

"Now unto him that is able to do exceeding abundantly above all that we ask or think, according to the power that worketh in us." (Ephesians 3:20)

I can remember thinking I have dreams and goals that I've been pressing toward for a long time, and I see others who really don't have a heart to heal make a mockery of broken women. I just want to make a difference. I never do anything on a small scale, it's always all or nothing! So, the refining process had to be more than I believed I could withstand. The effect of the things I am assigned to accomplish will make contributions spiritually and physically. This can only be done in excellence and I can't half-way do it. But Yah can see it through to completion.

And then it hit me. He doesn't showcase masterpieces on paper plates!

I was being prepared for such a time as this where there is a climate of confusion about what beauty is supposed to look like, a time where commercialism, false imagery, people hiding behind contoured faces and lace front weaves. Women and men alike are polishing the outside but living in spiritual bondage. A time where a generation of children are being raised by people with displaced purposes and unaware of their identity, a generation of people with no integrity brotherly/sisterly love and morals that are declining faster than a mudslide in Malibu.

The Bible talks about before the flood, like in the days of Noah. (Mark 24: 38) People were unaware of the calamity about to take place, so Yahua commanded Noah to start building this ark. Some laughed, ridiculed, and mocked the enormous structure because when asked why he was building it, he responded that a flood was coming and that water would fall from the heavens, since water had never fallen from the sky the people mocked Noah and said he was crazy. Yah watered the ground with the mist that came up from the earth.

"Now no shrub had yet appeared on the earth and no plant had yet sprung up, for Yahua Elohim had not sent rain on the earth and there was no one to work the ground, but streams came up from the earth and watered the whole surface of the ground." (Gen.2:5-6)

Oh, what the looks on their faces must have been when what he was proclaiming came true, and to find out that it was too late to undo the choice they had made about getting on board. Their choice to ignore the warning was detrimental to their entire families' existence.

Yah told Noah to build a protected place called an ark because he was going to cause a perfect storm. One that would cleanse the earth of those that had chosen to become enemies of their creator.

"Yah saw that the wickedness of man *was* great in the earth, and *that* every imagination of the thoughts of his heart *was* only evil continually." (Gen. 6:5)

Yah gave Noah this enormous task and for 120 years he pressed forward in ridicule and obscurity. But his obedience to what looked crazy to others created a platform and salvation for his family.

I am encouraged and I can dance in the storm because adversity has created a strength that only comes from the Creator. I am strong enough to know that nothing will kill me but death, so if I'm not dead, I have to push forward. The long wait was a prelude to the grand finale; the pain I endured and overcame was preparing me to recover from what most wouldn't survive. In retrospect, it takes courage to pause and look at pain from a new perspective to put on the mind of Mashiach and see life from the gardener's perspective. This made me take courage and embrace that all storms aren't to punish you, but you were chosen and trusted to grow and produce fruit that will bless others.

The evil that is sometimes bestowed on you by others can be the vehicle that is allowed to push you into your intended destination. What some people intend to harm you with Yahua can turn it into good. "But Joseph replied, "Do not be afraid. Am I in the place of Yah? As for you, what you intended against me for evil, Yah intended for good, in order to accomplish a day like this – to preserve the lives of many people. Therefore do not be afraid. I will provide for you and your little ones." So Joseph reassured his brothers and spoke kindly to them." (Gen. 50:19-21)

What would break others has shaped you, meaning you're the leader of the pack, you'll be the one to show others how to heal from the scars and wounds and carry on without packing excess baggage. They will take courage in doing so because you've done it. Without adversity, Joseph would not have saved Egyptians as well as, the nation of Israel would have starved to death and we wouldn't exist today.

Without adversity, Ruth would not have caught Boaz's attention. Ruth became David's grandmother. And David was Israel's second king. Esther would not have ended up in the Persian king's palace and saving the Hebrews from being annihilated. Esther was orphaned at birth, maybe because of war or famine. Esther was raised by her uncle Mordecai who taught her to love and revere the word of Elohim. This is evidence that some storms are a set up for Yah to showcase his masterpiece of a plan. Be encouraged and ride the storm, dance in the rain and learn a new song to sing in your tears.

"O sing unto Yah a new song; for he hath done marvellous things: his right hand, and his holy arm, hath gotten him the victory."(Psalms 98:1)

Take courage and know that your platform is being designed. And when you have overcome, your strength will be what others will draw from to ride out their storms. Yah created the adversary also and he has to get permission to touch those inside the hedge of Yah's protection meaning even he has to get permission to send a storm your way. What he doesn't know is he's being used to show the world how powerful your Creator really is.

A Day Late and a Dollar Short

"Do not boast about tomorrow, for you do not know what a day may bring."

(Proverbs 27:1)

Assuming that there will be time tomorrow for what's been put on your heart to do today, is one of Satan's greatest tools and biggest lies.

Procrastination made simple is failure to obey a prompting and is defiant. That gentle whisper to make a difference today was put in your spirit or consciousness by the Most High so to fail to promptly respond is disobedience and is very close to saying you know what is best for you at the time.

Delayed obedience is still disobedience and procrastination can lead to failure and distraction. When you start to look at time and realize that it is not afforded to many, you will start to have a whole new respect for the gift of right now. Right now, and immediate obedience are two of the most important things we have. Time is a gift that so many of us squander thinking that the opportunities and tasks that we are putting off today will be there tomorrow. Time really isn't on our side, in some cases, it really is working against us. We don't know the day nor the hour that our existence will cease. Neither do we know when the Creator will come and redeem his own and call the rest of creation into judgement.

So, the question is why do we waste time? Why do we spend time quarrelling, gossiping, and finding fault in others? When we should be applying every ounce of our existence doing what is pleasing to the Father. Shouldn't we participate in building up those that will carry on after we are gone?

Time is measured, one day is 24 hours, one week is seven days or 168 hours and one month is 30 days or 720 hours. Months are measured by the moon's cycles and one year is 365 days or 8760 hours. Now, let's observe this time concept; if it's measured, it must be precious. Also, if it is measured, it has a beginning and an ending. And the mystery of it all is we don't know when our time clock here will be up. We should manage it more wisely and quit acting like tomorrow is owed to us.

Time is not of the essence; it is fleeting and we are all but vapors. No one knows when they will be called to give an account for the deeds done in this body. Or to give account for the gifts that have been placed in their possession to share with the rest of creation. We all have tasks to complete while we occupy these earthly vessels.

It is such a shame to see people wandering aimlessly not taking full advantage of the small windows of opportunity they have to make lasting impressions in their children's lives, families' lives and people that have been placed in their realm of influence. It is such a disservice done to others for you to possess the possible antidote for their ailment and never share it. Whether that thing is love, compassion or time, it is extremely cruel to have the person in your presence and never give them what is free to give.

Most procrastinators are people who are controlled by their own narrative. And usually don't act on executing change until its often too late. I have witnessed the mother that wants to build a relationship with her children after she has gone their entire adolescence and wonder years not investing in their growth. I have seen the Father wanting a relationship with children after he decided he is lonely and none of the meaningless relationships he pursued were successful. I have witnessed the husband deciding he loves his wife and doesn't want to lose her after she has fallen out of love. All of these examples took time to happen. Each individual stated in my example thought that there would be time to make things right or change the course of direction. Time passes, children grow up and opportunities that were right in their grips have slipped away. Believing the sweet little lies that procrastination whispers in your ear can cost you more than you are willing to lose.

"And what do you benefit if you gain the whole world but lose your own soul?" (Mark 8:36)

Suddenly, after they realize the ball isn't in their court anymore, they want to jump into their feelings and give the people they neglected to love a guilt trip when, in all actuality, it is they who failed to use the small window of time they had to make a huge impact.

I have experienced this more times than I care to elaborate on. People who squandered opportunities and now they regret them. Knowing life transitions swiftly really should cause us to live intentional and with purpose.

"You, indeed, have made my days short in length, and my life span as nothing in Your sight. Yes, every mortal man is only a vapor. *Selah"*

(Psalm 39:5-6)

"Certainly, man walks about like a mere shadow. Indeed, they frantically rush around in vain, gathering possessions without knowing who will get them." (Psalms 39:5-6)

Purpose, as a noun, means the reason for which something is done or created, or for which something exists.

So many of us have not found what our purpose is and have delayed our own arrivals to our intended destinations in this life by procrastinating and making endless excuses for why we keep putting things off. Growth and elevation are supposed to be uncomfortable because you are entering a place of the unknown, and unfamiliar things can be very uncomfortable. But that's a good place to be; now, you can experience change.

We often settle for mediocrity and remain miserable because we are confined and imprisoned in our minds by the what-ifs! What if I fail? What if I look crazy to others doing this? What if you stay the same and in the same condition? That should be the most frightening!

Most of us don't know why we are wired the way we are and do a lot of what we do. A lot of it is generational and learned behaviors.

Someone before us did the same thing and we believed that was ok. Furthermore, we have listened to the lies that were passed down from generation to generation. You know the lies, you are not college material, you're not smart enough, pretty enough and this is just who we are. We were raised like this and this is who we are! Remember, just because things were done a certain way doesn't make the thing that is done right. Breaking generational curses requires recalibrating your thoughts about which direction you want to head in life. This is something that must be done as soon as you are aware of a deficiency in growth. When something is revealed to you, there are directions that should be followed without hesitation.

"Listen and hear my voice. Pay attention and hear what I say." (Isaiah 28:23)

When I speak of cursed, I don't mean in a magical, hocus-pocus kind of way, but almost trying to make something exist that doesn't have a form or any substance to it is equivalent to witchcraft. When we disobey truth and try to manipulate the order of operation, we can fall into misfortune.

We miss out on experiencing the very best that Yah had for us. Don't delay when a more excellent way is revealed.

Wearing Your Crown

"Though shalt be a royal crown of glory in the hand of
Elohim, and a royal diadem in the hand of your Yahua."

(Isaiah 62:3)

So many of us have been enamored with society's
view of what's beautiful and what's acceptable. We mimic
this by trying to live up to other people's expectations and
ideologies that claim to know what makes a woman worthy of
praise.

And with all these opinions and ideas we have still
missed the mark for years listening to what media, music and
society considers to be the virtue of a woman. We have people
mimicking words on pages and modeling after first ladies of
churches, rap and the music industry to still never really
experience what true transformation is. Being transformed
involves the truth. First, the truth about how you see yourself;
second, the truth about who you are and also what you haven't
become. Some have failed to arrive because of the level they
have chosen to operate on. We are told in scripture to be
imitators of the author and finisher of our faith.

118

"Therefore be imitators of Yah as beloved children; and walk in love, just as Mashiach also loved you and gave Himself up for us, an offering and a sacrifice to Yah as a fragrant aroma." (Ephesians 5:1-2)

We were not intended to be manufactured replicas of another woman. We are to be replicas of our Creator. Yah revealed himself and did so under full disclosure not withholding any good thing from those that love him and obey him. And that you are doing so under full disclosure and transparency. If not, you will find yourself entangled in the spider's web of confusion and in the lost and found looking for your crown, and the one you will end up wearing may not even be yours.

The truth is most of these women are only revealing what they want you to see. They want you to see the crown on their head but won't tell you the raw organic truth or the recipe to wearing your own crown unapologetically. We are all created in the image of Yah and he has given us all distinct gifts and a portion of boldness. Boldness to navigate through this life living out our purpose in His truth.

"For Yah hath not given us the spirit of fear; but of power, and of love, and of a sound mind." (2 Timothy 1:7)

They believe by omitting the pain, mistakes, fake friends and heartache that are all involved with obtaining the crown will keep them in position to sit higher than you. But the truth of the matter is a lot of respect is lost when it all comes out in the wash and you realize that you have been mimicking an illusion, a whitewashed tomb.

They will direct you to address scripture to only leave you more confused, like 1 Peter 3:3-4: "Don't let your adorning be external" (scripture paraphrased) to only leave you lost and thinking you shouldn't be grooming and enhancing the attributes Yahua gave you when there is so much more to why this message was even being preached. Culture and context of conversations are very important as to why truth and knowing the point of reference to arrival is also.

In this life, we never truly arrive. We can elevate but it doesn't just happen by waking up one day and saying, "I have it all figured out and abracadabra I have it all together!"

No, it happened over years. It happened by failing the test with flying colors and giving in to impulses and having to recover from epic embarrassments and failures. That is why it looks like some women are unbreakable, it's because they have already been broken and restored and Yah has restored the brokenness into a mosaic masterpiece and they aren't afraid to share it.

Women who refuse to operate in full disclosure or transparency often create minions and not disciples or daughters of Sarah or Hannah. They really aren't facilitating women into becoming strong individual queens but are creating a cultic group of parishioners that worship a false leader.

Queens don't let what another has said about another queen dictate whether she likes them or not, she allows their actions to speak toward their character and lives in a way that will promote trust in the Creator and will be the solid foundation of other queens' castles. Mentors are equivalent to what the Bible calls having wise counsel. Wisdom equips the queen who is unsure of the materials she needs to build her tools.

"Through wisdom a house is built, And by understanding it is established; By knowledge the rooms are filled with all precious and pleasant riches. A wise man *is* strong, Yes, a man of knowledge increases strength;

For by wise counsel you will wage your own war,
And in a multitude of counselors *there is* safety." (Proverbs
24:3-6)

A queen wears her crown because she has realized that
she is fully known and loved by her creator. The recipe for
who she was destined to become came included at her time of
arrival to this universe. She has realized that she always
radiated the posture and a presence of a queen all her life.
Others could see the components she possessed and wondered
why she couldn't see what caused others to marvel.

All of her life people have tried to connect to her to
pull from the power she possessed and hadn't quite owned
herself. She has always possessed something others knew they
lacked and since her heart is big, kind and full of love, others
wanted to draw it from her.

Once she eventually realizes that all along, she has
been acting as the accessory that added the finishing touch to
other's entire look and many of the people whom she graced
with her presence never even deserved for her to be there.
Growth has helped her to embrace being the total outfit and
loving it. Life is all about evolution and it is a journey of
learning and growth that can be a never-ending fountain of
knowledge and an asset to others, if we are willing to share

what we have learned from our travels through time, failures and growth.

As soon as you omit one component of your evolving, you remove who you are, and it causes those that are looking for a path to follow to be deviated by a lie. To operate in secrecy and pride robs the ones whom have been placed in your realm of influence.

Real people love real people and when you have mastered the art of introspection and keeping it real where you live at, it's simple to keep it real with others. Secrets and lies only have as much power as you invest in trying to keep them covered. Own and embrace you and your journey and exist in the power of you.

Wearing your crown begins with embracing who you are and where you have been, because there is no one like you! I have learned from my past and I am motivated by my failures. The only thing I regret is never trying.

You will be fine if you continue to move forward and not look back because you aren't going in that direction. **"I press toward the mark for the prize of the high calling of Elohim in Yeshua Hamashiach. Let us therefore, as many as be perfect, be thus minded: and if in any thing ye be otherwise minded, Elohim shall reveal even this unto you."**

(Philippians 3:14)

And if you continue to progress driving backwards you will continue to collide with the things that are meant to stay behind you. Proceed forward but never go before The Most High, which most do that confess to follow him.

We were created to commune and to be relational and love and care for one another; this is paramount to existence. No one can prosper or grow alone because you need accountability and love as well as encouragement to manifest. Truth and protection as well as transparency are so important. Being relational involves telling some painful truths and uncovering some ugly hurts, because the common denominator of relationships should be about love and trust. Once truth is embraced, even the ugly has some humor in it, but as long as you deny and cover, you permeate and create a stench of discord and delusion.

You also must be careful about whom you will choose to commune with and really pick your circle that will be able to dine from your table as you cast pearls of wisdom. Being relational involves two parties that have things in common that will challenge growth and encourage each other to become better at reaching their full potential. Love covers a multitude of shortcomings and real queens adjust one another's crowns.

"Therefore confess your sins to each other and pray for each other so that you may be healed. The prayer of a righteous person is powerful and effective." (James 5:16)

The things that you have been allowed to come through are your own unique narrative to the making of you. Your ETA is on a divine timeline and the only thing that stands in most people's way is themselves. I mean repeating cycles that keep rendering the same outcome and disobedience to what has been revealed to you by the experience. Staying engaged with women who refuse to grow can distract you if you engage or entertain their foolery too long. Don't allow foolery and disobedience to micromanage your journey.

So, it almost seems like a bad joke to hide truth, masked in deceit and darkness and watch a young lady filled with purpose and no direction scramble, stumble and fall looking for her recipe for her crown when you have the oracle that will help her unlock it.

It is the biggest act of hypocrisy to omit hurt, pain and failures, coupled with bad choices, when grooming a queen. Lies can send a person in the obscure direction of repeating the same mistakes you made. Putting on masks will not help a woman to become what they perceive you to be. Learning to master a disguise is manipulating the order of operation. This is close to causing one to believe in magic. Not being truthful can send a person who admires you to go looking for imaginary things. Don't become one who is guilty of giving a false sense of hope to a woman who trusts you. Wearing a mask won't bring a sister to the destination she is hoping to arrive at, especially when it is worn by a person they are looking to help guide them to a productive and fruitful end. We are all spiritual beings having a human experience, and Yah is the lamp unto our feet and a light unto our path. He created us with a vacuum in our heart. The heart in Hebrew is (leb) and the word means the seat of our emotions. In the seat of our emotions we are longing for a connection; one that will guide us to our purpose in life. Well, we know that the only one who knows this purpose is our creator, but in his love and providence he will set some divine appointments. These divine appointments will connect us with one that is connected to Him.

"Your word *is* a lamp to my feet and a light to my path." (Psalm 119:110)

I'm not telling you to have a confession session with every woman you meet; that would be absurd. I am saying that we are all in a realm that operates cyclically, and people are sent our way by divine design. The universe has a distinct way of letting you know when your assignment has come your way. When this moment happens, it is your chance to pour out all of the pearls of wisdom that have been entrusted to you.

We have to convey to our youth that we are more than strippers, hoes and booty calls, baby mommas and drama queens.

We are the creators of life and the glue that holds families together. It's obvious that a lot of queens don't know this because they embrace a culture and a lie portrayed by others. We have to continue to encourage young queens that we can be the glue that holds a generation together or we can be the storm that destroys homes and generations. Don't be the one that comes into a woman who is seeking directions in life and depict and nurture ignorance and a love for foolishness.

A lot of women have inherited the pain passed down for generations of wounded queens with stepped on crowns. The truth is so many women that are supposed to be leading and showing other ladies how to successfully queen, are suffering from the absence of encouragement. These women didn't experience love and praise that they so desired from their nurturers as they were supposed to be learning how to queen up. Now we have the elders lacking pearls of wisdom to drop to the youth, and then blaming them for not knowing how to act. And the youth are looking to the youth for answers and the equation is unbalanced and not adding up. We have a whole generation of deficient women incapable of loving correctly, unable to exercise self-control, and chasing boys, marrying grown boys while raising boys and not kings. We have women raising grown little girls and not queens because they lack the main ingredients that are needed for healthy adults: love, security and nurturing that produces confidence.

Inside of every woman is a little girl looking for the love that wasn't cultivated at crucial times and stages in her life. This happens either by parents not being aware or by lack of awareness of their child's personality. However, the deficit took place, the time is now for every man/woman to stop reliving and perpetuating trauma and break vicious cycles.

Most parents who have failed horribly at parenting say that children don't come with instructions and when you hear a parent say that, it's usual because they failed to read the instructions that came with life. In this instruction book that parents say children don't come with there is this regurgitated passage that every parent I have encountered knows to quote; some of the most unorthodox parents I know can quote this one scripture, "Honor your mother and father son that your days will be long upon the earth." (Exodus 20:12, Ephesians 6:2) This book is called the Torah, and the entire book contains instructions on how to be in relationship with our Creator, leadership, the universe and most of all one another. So, to make the statement that there are no instructions on how to love and raise children speaks of a cruel creator.

No manufacturer created a device and left you without an owner's manual, unless it was a bootleg and then you could still search Google or YouTube and see how to operate it. So, it's safe to say that instructions were given somewhere along, and some parents failed to read them or adhere to them.

We have been left with wisdom and knowledge in Torah. The Most High invites us to try him and learn from him and he will not lead you into crafty counsel but will lead you into all truth.

If you were the little girl that needed a hug or desired to be told that she was beautiful, capable and smart, He has a message for you and will divinely set up some appointments for you to meet some recovered queens along the way to walk this path with you.

Most grown women have been ridiculed, estranged, broken and are longing for the love that only the Creator can supply them. "To appoint unto them that mourn in Zion, to give unto them beauty for ashes, the oil of joy for mourning, the garment of praise for the spirit of heaviness; that they might be called trees of righteousness, the planting of the LORD, that he might be glorified." (Isaiah 61:3)

I am grateful to the queens in my life who have loved me and trusted me and allowed me to witness their transfiguration. Transfiguration is a complete change of form or appearance into a more beautiful and spiritual state. These ladies have been a safe place and we have learned to love each other even when it was hard to like each other. I am able to share because they were transparent with me in their season of purging. I pray my truth encourages you along your way.

A queen can only stand as tall and as strong as her roots sink. Healthy roots and a strong foundation are very important for young queens in training. If there is bad fruit, it doesn't always mean the roots are bad but the season the tree weathered hindered the production of good fruit. This tree requires pruning a cutting of the scarred branches to allow healthy ones to grow and bear good fruit. Only a master gardener knows which branches need to be pruned. Once pruned and the tree doesn't produce fruit, then it's safe to say the roots are bad. At this point, a removal of the tree is necessary. Being pruned is a humbling experience but the posture of a student or vessel should always be one of humility. This is where the one who can make provisions is able to lean in and gently minister and encourage you.

Knowing your worth will allow you to stay the course. Looking to the author and finisher of your journey. There is a generation that has distorted what being a true woman of royalty is. It's not being a bad bitch; a bitch is a female dog and they run in packs and do what dogs do. I will allow you to use your own imagination about what that is. It's not sleeping with men for a bag, or a trip. Neither is it sleeping with a man that has made no commitment to you and sending him on his way. This is whoredom! Remember that a person cannot give you what they don't have.

Queens come through storms with her shoulders back and her head held high. She can still walk to your room and command attention because there is hope in her heart and a strength in her stride as well as a song in her smile.

She rules because she has mastered being herself. She learned to love her journey mistakes and all, she recovered, is better from them and doesn't cry over spilled milk. She has learned to trust in the promises of her Creator.

"Though your beginning was small, Yet your latter end would increase abundantly." (Job 8:7)

Hurting People Hurt People; Protecting and Guarding is Real Love

"A friend loves at all times, and a brother is born for a time of adversity."

(Proverbs 17:17)

Seeking wise counsel and constituents are important because spectators are always looking to catch you walking with your crown on crooked or waiting for an opportunity to knock it off and expose your shortcomings. Usually, when a sister is injured or caught off guard by betrayal, it is because someone within the circle of trust has allowed an intruder to infiltrate and rob the relationship of protected knowledge and precious gems that took years to secure. Like shared moments about your deepest fears or the details to your failing marriage or maybe just a vent that was only spoken to help you bring things back into perspective.

The word states that evil will never leave the house of the one who pays back evil for good.

Inside jobs are the worst because it reveals dishonor, betrayal and a lack of concern for everyone in the compound.

Innocent people always suffer because of selfish people's desires or lack of discretion and self-control. The need to know and then divulge what you know reveals so much about a person's character, and no matter what disguise the person who is a betrayer comes masked behind, the real them will show up eventually. Wolves clothe themselves in sheep's clothing in order to gain access to those who are vulnerable. Once the wolf is amongst the flock of sheep, that wolf can be dangerous. People allowed into your life that lack honor and loyalty are as dangerous as a wolf in sheep's clothing.

Everyone should have a safe place to be human, meaning vulnerable, a sounding board and some place where truth is spoken to them or they can reveal some hard truths, and it stays right there. As women, we have so many other components in life that stress and strain us, and the last thing we should have to do when we are around one another is to feel like we are in combat. "A friend loves at all times, and a brother is born for adversity." (Prov. 17:17)

It is so sad how stereotypes about our community of women are only negative. We are always cantankerous, argumentative and gossipy. If I see one more *Love and Hip Hop* reunion, *Basketball Wives*, or *Housewives* show exploiting and promoting dysfunction within the community of melanated women I will start collecting signatures to get a vote on the ballot to boycott these shows! These women, beautifully lavished in expensive gowns and faces "beat to the gods" with hair coiffed and precisely placed while they are speaking to each other like they just stepped off the USS Constitution. Queens behaving like savages, throwing shoes and popping off nails like they were raised by wolves, for a dollar, I will just scream.

There is so much more to us (women of color) than foolery and ignorance. We should be portraying love and community and showing our youth and the ones looking for direction something wholesome and healing so that the world sees that we love our children, husbands and one another. All of us aren't being beaten or cheated on and ignorant.

There has to be some wise women amongst us that will stand and set in motion the positive portrait of us as queens, rulers, confidants and advisers. We have to think about the eternal riches of healing a nation of women instead of a few dollars for some new shoes, a leather bag and a trip. We exploit each other for fame but we forget the women before us that invested morals, values and love into each other and children that weren't even theirs so that we could progress to higher ground.

We as women have adopted such a Eurocentric slave mentality and we take on so many things that we have forgotten who we are. Nation builders. "A stone of stumbling and a rock of offense. They stumble because they disobey the word—and to this they were appointed. "But you are a chosen people, a royal priesthood, a holy nation, a people for Yah's own possession, to proclaim the virtues of Him who called you out of darkness and into his marvelous light. Once you were not a people, but now you are the people of Yah; once you had not received mercy, but now you have received mercy." (1 Peter 2:9-10)

Do you remember that it was our ancestors that nursed and groomed our slavers' children and taught them manners? Our slavers taught us that we were lazy savages while we worked seven days a week with minimal resources and inhumane living quarters. Observation has showed us that we are survivors, conquerors and more than resilient. We are so convoluted and confused we didn't come from broken homes. The brokenness came from being stolen and dispersed. Our culture being stolen and covered. The concept of not claiming and caring for our children happened on the plantation when the slavers raped the slave woman and the slave's husband couldn't contest because that would end in death. The slaver didn't claim his children and left a broken man and woman to raise and care for a child conceived in an act of violence. We were said to not love our children and that couldn't have been farther from the truth. We loved our masters' children and ours. Our men, before being denied the right to be a man, took care of their women and children. The disconnect and self-hatred all happened during the diaspora and we still glorify the pain and ignorance for currency. We have to stop!

We are supposed to be the standard; the template for other women to follow.

We should not be driven to divulge everything a sister shares with us to the next women, the fact that a person trusts you enough to divulge should be reason enough for you to guard it. I'd rather be trusted than popular for knowing everything and telling it. Remember where much is given, much is required, and because the people of the diaspora (melanated) community are leading in mental health, drug abuse and incarceration you should consider that if a person vents and gets things off their hearts and minds that may be saving them from their breaking point. However, what do you do? Tell it? Wrong! We need to guard, protect and heal one another. Community is a part of divine design and essential for survival. "A brother offended is harder to be won than a strong city: and their contentions are like the bars of a castle." (Prov. 18:19)

I am not saying we don't disagree and not see eye to eye, what I'm saying is let's learn to say what we mean to each other in love and even if it's hurtful, respect each other's perspective and love and heal past it. The whole world shouldn't see what happens in house. Again, I never promote hiding abuse whether its mentally, physically or emotionally—there are some non-negotiable behaviors. We as women are nation builders and our nation and community are only as strong as we are holistically.

Excommunication is a must when its injurious and uncovers and poses as a weak link in the chain of the sisterhood. This can infect the whole community of the sisterhood and cause a division, get rid of the one who likes to divide. "These six *things* Yahua hates, Yes, seven *are* an abomination to Him: A proud look, A lying tongue, Hands that shed innocent blood, A heart that devises wicked plans, Feet that are swift in running to evil, A false witness *who* speaks lies, And one who sows discord among brethren." (Prov. 6:16-19)

Women are the strong leaders and the current that moves the direction of the family. Either hell has no fury like a woman scorned or the hand that rocks the cradle rules the world, meaning a woman can make a house a warm and beautiful place to be in or she can make it hell on earth.

Start looking at what is being done by the powers that be to our families when we believe we are supposed to live up to these personas that we see foolish women building fame to a whole community's complete demise.

Women should behave and treat each other like one amongst equals. There is no high and lifted up and low or worthless women. There are some that are misdirected and foolish and the approach to waking a sleepwalker is to be very carefully. We all are born with purpose and design, some just haven't been helped to combine the recipe for the making of a strong, beautiful you.

Discernment is always necessary when you are allowing someone in your space though, and with this being stated, Yahua gave us five senses. We need to use them. Everyone isn't ready for community because they have been injured and all they know how to do is injure others. People don't care how much you know until they know how much you care; this is why we need to shift gears and lead instead of tearing down each other.

Let's learn to celebrate each other and support one another. When a sister is struggling, reach your hand out to help her up not step on her neck and make it harder for her to get up. Tell her you see her striving and working to reach her goals; encourage and acknowledge her and tell her that one day it'll pay off. Never stop pressing toward her goal, never stop hoping, never stop loving, keep believing in truth and the ability to dream is a gift that Yahua has placed in her heart and dreams do come to fruition. Most women have one thing in common, that is we all are connected whether we like to admit it or not. We all love and want to be loved. Learn when sharing is edifying and when it is too much or a prelude to a mess. We all have the power to create good or bad. We are life-givers, nurturers and builders. Some just haven't had their purpose for design cultivated and nurtured correctly.

When you know how to cover and protect, you have either been privileged to be nurtured by a mother or surrogate who has decided she wasn't going to repeat vicious cycles that tear down. Or you were left uncovered and unprotected and you know how this feels; you have decided to be a safe place for sisters.

In order to heal, you have to be willing to approach life with a mask off attitude. You have to quit living in fear of being rejected, hurt and daring enough to not care how people will perceive you for being brave enough to be transparent and serious enough about setting boundaries that have specific off-limit areas for people who are habitual line-steppers.

Women who protect have fought some battles and some battles have left some scars that most can't see. However, she has chosen to use the battle wounds to remind her that she is alive and what didn't kill her pushed her into her destiny.

Scars are marks from a fight she thought she wouldn't recover from or the emptiness she felt after she walked away from the love that was never returned. She chose to build on the injury that was inflicted, and she applied the hurt to her life in a different fashion, it didn't kill her, so she chose to make others stronger.

We need to learn how to walk in the room with confidence and poise and that it takes nothing away from you to honor and address another beautiful woman with love and respect. This is another building tactic that makes others wonder where you got the power to own and love yourself.

This power source is endless, for all we are required to do is point others in that direction.

Growth and maturity are exhibited when you spread the love and joy you have discovered to other women. Offer a smile to a sister and complement her on her beauty, we are all of the Creators creation.

Learn to love people where they are right now even though they may not be on the same frequency that you are on now. Love will be the motivation that will inspire her to accelerate. We are all on a journey and everyone doesn't reach the final destination at the same time, some must go ahead of others to light the path for those coming after her.

Knowing that silence is king and reigns supreme and that fear is loud will save you from a lot of unnecessary misquotes. Wisdom is poised and calculated, it knows when to address an issue and when to just observe.

A lot of quarrels and fights can be put to rest when we learn there are no points to prove because each woman's metamorphosis comes by the hand of her Creator and when she decides to submit to obedience.

I have learned just because something is silent doesn't mean that they are not powerful, have you witnessed the power of a tsunami? Or an earthquake? Their forces can be deadly and its without warning.

Learning to be as wise as a serpent and as harmless as a dove comes from listening and observing more than you desire to be heard.

Humility has everything to do with growing up.

Wisdom became wise by not forgetting the paths that lead her to places she never wants to visit again, young sisters listen to instruction and are rescued and lead out of darkness by observing a survivor that has gone before you.

Lean in close enough to hear her voice and then listen to her and do not respond. I have experienced a lot of dialogue being had where people are listening to respond but not listening to hear what is being said. These results are a lot of talk and both parties walking away still drawing their own conclusions but still not communicating on a common foundation. A change cannot come if we don't reason one with another and learn to respect being women, having differences and still learn to love and respect one another in our differences.

On your journey, don't become distracted by the static of those that are not cheering for you, realize that everything isn't for everybody, and that what is for you is given to you by Yah.

Only you can say what needs to be said about you. If you don't write your own story others will do a crappy job at conveying to the world what was in your heart. Don't allow people to try to set the standard for who they believe that you are, you show them who you are by shattering the glass ceilings other people's narratives have placed in your way.

In this life, we are on assignment from the Most High and the objective is to touch lives. We may not have taken the most conventional routes, some may have been very colorful and laced with a lot of controversy. Yah reminds us that He can use even our days in the dark to manifest a masterpiece.

To some, most of the time life seems like it may be a spectator's sport but it isn't. Everyone has a position to play but not many want to get in and give it a shot because they are so busy waiting to see how it will work out for you.

Use your gifts. If that gift is a heart for other women, then encourage and inspire them. Take a young queen searching by the hand and walk the dark paths and low roads with her and direct her to well-lighted paths and higher planes. Coming into the knowledge of the fact that we don't all perform for the same audience or dance to the same song as everyone else is so liberating. And that although we all have different songs, when we unite in truth and love with the women placed on our frequency, the sound can be vainglorious.

We have such a small amount of time to make large investments in the life of those coming up after us and to leave a first impression on those who you grace with your presence. There should be an urgency to deposit healthy seeds and nurture and protect them until their roots are strong enough not to be ripped out of good soil.

Life is cyclical and you will always meet people again on this journey. What is the one thing you want people to remember about their encounter with you? Rest assured, one impression that is lasting is how you made them feel when you were in their presence.

Operating in truth, righteousness, fairness and integrity will keep you blameless. Keep your closet free of skeletons because we know the devil loves secrets and loves to wreak havoc behind the scenes when he can keep you suppressing truth and hiding lies. That is a sure tactic that will keep you from assuming your position as a healer and owning your calling.

No matter what you do you will have opposition, whether you like it or not, press harder toward your goal because opposition means you're on to something good.

People will either love you or they will hate you and just because some people desire to be in your presence doesn't mean they are ready for who you are. You aren't for everyone and everyone's company isn't meant for you. Be vigilant against the attack of those that come to either drain you or distract you. With the unsurmountable amount of pain our women and community are in, distractions are the last thing you need. Some people are like moths to flames but they cannot handle the light you possess, they either ignite and catch on fire and can burn you in the process. Light can show them their imperfections and show them where they need to step up to life's plate, but instead of taking what is revealed and applying to their situation for the purpose of changing, they make excuses as to why they can't elevate and despise you for having the courage to grow.

Be really selective about the company you keep and the things you share with others because someone that is afraid of change is always looking for ammunition to shoot you with. Most of the time we have supplied them with the ammunition because we offered them a seat at our table.

Don't give others bullets for their guns to use against you, know when to share to edify and when to observe to study whether you are in the company of your enemy or a friend.

Most people are really selective about their sympathies, so save your dime and be careful about who you dialogue and share your story with, as you know that where much is given much more is required, some can't be trusted with much and their lifestyle will rat them out.

The most important agenda is to leave something for the next woman coming to glean. Share with them a morsel of soul food, drop a nugget of wisdom showing the up and coming sister how to walk, how to talk, how to position herself and most of all about how to seek truth and share it.

Finding Shalom with No Shalem

"The worst part about being angry at a person is being angry
and not being able to do anything about it."

~ Nia Marie

This chapter is for everyone growing bitter waiting on apologies or restitution to be paid for the offenses that have been inflicted upon you. If we are transparent and keep it real where we live at, we can all attest to the fact that some of our strongest convictions have been birthed out of our deepest hurts or our darkest secrets. Many of us are holding ourselves hostage to the perceived thoughts that you thought others harbored toward you and give imagined thoughts free rental space in our minds. We are offended by social media posts and lose sleep over subliminals that aren't intended for us. Holding on to negative energy toward others while they sleep peaceful at night.

Some of us have lived for what seems like an eternity with feelings of inadequacy that took root because we have allowed ourselves to stay in a bad situations long past the expiration date. We want closure that will never come with answers.

Once you have decided to walk in light and truth, you free yourself from the chains that the anticipation of an apology and the burdens that others in pain will try to inflict on you. While you are healing from injury, the one thing you believe will help you heal is for the offending party to say sorry and if you just received that you would be ok. Not true. Healing is within you; you can set yourself free from the pain of waiting for an apology.

Once you realize that most people who inflict injury and excuse the behavior are bound by pride and a lack of accountability, and you waiting on retribution from these people is like putting on shackles and throwing away the key. Learn to deal in reality and not expectations; you will have more peace because of it. I have had the revelation that people that harm others are weak and hurting and to let go of the power they feel their disposition possesses will leave them powerless. Sadly, this may be true, admitting where they wronged another will leave them without leverage to feel strong by inflicting injury.

Life is about evolution and change. You shouldn't be the same person you were at 18 now that you are 28, nor should you be the same person you were when you're 30. You shouldn't act like a 20-year-old, it just doesn't add up and isn't attractive. I have witnessed it though, men and women overgrown but still walking around with the hurt feelings of a five-year-old because of unresolved hurt.

Some people literally lack the capacity to empathize and I wish I had come to grips with this sooner than later, it would have saved me a lot of wasted energy and anger.

The only time an inflictor can see what their offenses feel like is when they are committed to them. I call this "doing a you on you!" Offenders operate by something I call the "backwards mirror ministry," possessing the capacity to see what others do but never having the ability to see what causes others pain. These people literally lack compassion and the ability to see their faults and why others respond to them the way they do. Many lack the capacity to be introspective, because it requires courage to change.

They have learned to do this because admitting offenses means you are wrong and saying sorry when they are wrong requires laying down pride as well as learning a new way to operate. Unchartered territory is fearful but if it's to build and edify, it's worth the try. Pride is the armor that a person who demands their own way wears. A prideful person must feel like their way is the best way even if it is at the expense of destroying another person's peace. This mindset is traumatizing and crippling because it causes others to resent and disdain the person who won't admit when they have wronged someone.

Love involves empathy, protection, and the desire to equip the object of your affection with the tools to render unto you the same love and treatment you want from them. An obstinate person acts as if they don't care if you loathe them or not because if it is negative energy they receive, it's better than nothing, they can use it because their frequency is on empty.

If we watch the universe, we will see that everything it does involves cycles of reciprocity. You get out what you put in. Life has a cycle; plants have a cycle as the seasons and the atmosphere do too.

So, it is only fair to say that as far as being relational we should mimic the universe also. If I want good from a relationship then I should deposit good into it, right? This is what makes me wonder why so many live by a different code? I have observed that people raised where love was invested operate different in life than those that were raised on survival. Those raised on survival have a survival-of-the-fittest, dog-eat-dog mentality, even toward those that have shown them love. And more times than I would like to admit, I have loved and invested in people before I paid attention to who they really were. All because I believe that if I show love and treat you how I want to be treated this will be reciprocated. Needless to say, I have learned some painful lessons subscribing to this way of thinking.

I have loved the one that takes and doesn't replace, I do harm and want good to come to me and how dare anyone hold me accountable for my actions. I stayed while being treated less than I knew I deserved because I made excuses for them. I had come to the conclusion that I was going to get something out of my many investments until it almost cost me my wellbeing. He owed me for the years of love I invested, for bearing with his embarrassing behaviors, and monetary investments I made early on in our relationship. I believed eventually, the light would click on and something would manifest from the love and care I had invested in him. That was a lie so I decided that I couldn't heal in the same space that caused me injury and I left no apology and all behind. Hard as it may be or as it sounds, we as women need to love ourselves enough to know when to exit a toxic, fruitless relationship.

Based on my experience the only time the people I have encountered are capable of wanting to be sorry is when calamity is pointing its sights in their direction. Other than that, they operate by looking out of windows and focusing on what they see, never taking the time to set their sights internally and see why they inflict injury on people they profess to love.

So many of us suffer from brokenness, disappointment, deceit, even self-infliction because of the vacuums in our hearts that long to be filled with the love we crave. The need to be validated by the person that hurt us can spill over into other relationships in our lives. If we don't heal from our last traumatic experience, we will keep attracting others that possess the same character flaws and inflict more injury on ourselves looking for love and healing.

We have strained relationships with mothers and absent relationships from fathers and haven't been able to get over it because we keep attracting incomplete individuals into our space.

"Get over it " has become a standard reply of people who offend you and want to stay in your space. They need you to sweep the last offense under the rug so that they can get started on the next offense. You can't heal if a person remains present and continues to pick at your scabs. It is ok to be alone; it is ok to breathe, it is ok to process how you arrived at a place and formulate a plan of wellness and no matter who the person is that has offended: mother, father, sister, brother or mate, distance and strong boundaries are necessary for your recovery.

While I remained in the storm of my fragmented marriage, all I could focus on was ducking for cover and bracing myself for what may potentially come next. This made me anxious and tired. Yah allowed and orchestrated an open door that allowed me to step out of my storm so that I could see the objects that were flying around that would eventually kill me.

We are not required to be a doormat or dump truck for another person's sickness and pain.

The first part of forgiveness required me to forgive myself for allowing the mistreatment I allowed in different relationships. Next, I did some unpacking of boxes I had stored in my heart. I had to sort through the "whys." Why did I allow certain behaviors? What made me stay? Why was I angry at them for doing what I allowed? The truth, I discovered, was that I was afraid that someone else would reap the benefits of all the time and love that I had invested in this relationship. Then I realized it only worked because I was forcing myself to live in dysfunction. I had convinced myself to exist in an unhealthy environment waiting for retribution that would never come or be sincere. In this particular case, this person was only sorry when I wasn't there to feed their ego.

Indoctrination and people not willing to face their faults believe forgiveness to be a magic word. Forgiveness requires the offended party to cover the offense, but the guilty party must take action also. The guilty party must be willing to not inflict the same offense or injury on the victim again. I know I was taught that if a person asks for forgiveness you get over it and give it to "god." But there is really more .

Let's examine judicial law first. I look at the way our system is set up; people who commit offenses are required to pay a debt for the crime committed to the one they have committed the crime against and sometimes even serve a sentence of incarceration, or probation. And even if you have been pardoned of the crime by a judge, you should never want to find yourself before the judge for the same crime, would you? This would show a lack of regard for the forgiving authority. Try not paying a court ordered fine placed on the records and watch them garnish your wages and levy your accounts and your tax returns until the debt is paid in full. If this is required in everyday moral law, what do you think the creator of the universe and his spiritual laws require? "And Yahua spoke to Moses, saying, 'Speak to the people of Israel, When a man or woman commits any of the sins that people commit by breaking faith with the Yahua, and that person realizes his guilt, he shall confess his sin that he has committed. And he shall make full restitution for his wrong, adding a fifth to it and giving it to him to whom he did the wrong.'" (Numbers 5:5-7)

You can't change the act, but the act of being willing to submit something you earn to compensate the persons pain shows intent to mend the situation. Trust may take time to be built again but it's easier to respect a person who tries to repair what they have broken, than one who is driven by pride.

The situation is the same when it comes to love and family, forgive and forgetting isn't reality. I can say I forgive but I can't forget if you don't put forth the effort to change the behaviors that offend. In some cases, love and fellowship can be restored and, in some cases, moving on is the best prescription. Not making a person aware of what they have done to you can make them think it's okay. But what they do with what you have revealed to them and how they offended you is now up to them. You cannot make a person heal you, the responsibility and choice to heal is all yours.

It's such an oppressive mentality to want honor respect and love from the very person you offend, murder and oppress, and never pay restitution or compensate for what you have robbed them of.

I have come in contact with so many people that have repressed pain and have turned to sex, drugs and suffered mental illness behind this way of thinking. We become that which we meditate on.

We've been so miseducated when it comes to forgiveness and the steps that follow; first there has to be an admission of guilt. Then you must ask for forgiveness and to be honestly sorry you must not intentionally commit the act again. After offenses have been forgiven; the way to continue in a relationship is to turn away from behaviors that break fellowship.

We cannot fellowship with brokenness, it's a cancer that continues to eat away at both parties. The one who offended wonders when you will give them what they know they deserve and the offended one is always waiting around guarding because they are waiting for the offender to strike again.

This alone can make a person crazy!

However, there comes a point in time where pain must stop and healing takes place. To pretend I'm not offended about being hurt or to pretend that something never happened to me is as painful as the injury in the first place.

It's amazing how one little word can possess the power to set one free or hold them captive. This one little word can cast a spell or break what seems like a curse. It can cast a spell, because we say it and have no actions behind the word to back it up and we will create illusions. Illusions that they are sorry because they stick around, they just hang around to rob you of your joy.

Used in all sincerity, the word sorry can mend fences and heal years of pain, but withheld and avoided, this word has the power to make you feel devalued, and frustrated. It's true that to heal and be reconciled one must have some form of closure, in a perfect world all would get what they seek. But when it never comes, do some closing of the doors to portals that can inflict further injury to yourself.

Sorry shows that you possess the capacity to feel the distress of another's misfortune, and that can be quite hard when you are the one who caused it. Reality can be stranger than fiction and life can make you wonder if some of this mess is made up. Life is a rehearsal for one big production, you learn as you go, use even the disappointments as a tool to be better. Now, this is when we get to the good part.

This chapter is for everyone growing bitter waiting on apologies or restitution to be paid for the offenses that have been inflicted upon you. This is for the woman who can't move forward because of the apology they have been waiting on to release them from the invisible chains of anger. You have been free all along, you just needed to know you aren't the only one. Release.

Be ok with it not happening, everyone isn't capable of dealing with their own inadequacies or capable of dealing with their short comings enough to validate your hurt. I did it, so can you.

We have been so miseducated when it comes to forgiveness and the steps that follow the admission of guilt and asking for forgiveness. We use the word like it's witchcraft. Say sorry and move on and everything is fixed.

Band-Aids don't fix bullet wounds; surgery does, and if a person cares about you enough they will go under the knife and have things that hurt or offend removed. Don't keep letting injured and dying folk who refuse to seek healing make you sick.

Love is supposed to bring balance and healing. When a person refuses to allow you to heal and love yourself enough to grow and elevate. Know that I love you, know that I'm sorry for the ones who never apologized to you. Know that I'm praying with you and for you in your healing.

I know that I have never believed a lie that I didn't want to be the truth. Neither have I ever excused away the truth that I didn't want to believe. See, we all possess that capacity to move into a place called cognitive dissonance where we see the way something is operating or being executed but we trust the voice in our head that tells us what we want to hear. Sometimes we have to step away from a situation to really see the big picture and that's when I have often realized I was bigger than the picture and was trying to make myself fit where I had outgrown.

No one will love you like you love you; be healed, be whole, be restored.

Broken People Break People

"Be not dismayed bad company corrupts good morals."

(1 Cor. 15:33)

Birds of a feather flock together is what I have always been told and the statement has been proven to be so true. Observational evidence is more true than most people care to admit. You have police officers, social workers, psychiatrists, doctors and lawyers that want to repair and fix and protect the ones that lack resources, that are emotionally scarred, the ones that have been psychologically injured and socially oppressed.

Then you have mentors, teachers, and foster parents that want to help shape, direct and influence those that have been misguided or have had no direction given to them at all. And all of these people have one thing in common; they have either been the one that was harmed, or they witnessed injustice or harm happen either in their family or by observing the ways of the world and decided to make a change. We call these people the ones who have taken lemons and made lemonade.

Then you have the ones who have never quite been capable to let go and operate because of the trauma that they experienced or because they have become so familiar with their brokenness that they perpetuate the cycle. Broken people believe they are ok where they are; this is a sad but so true, a frame of mind that a lot of people exist in.

Yes, I use the term existing because it's not living, yet so many people believe that it is. And when you try to help lead them out of their familiar place, they offer excuses and reasons for why they stay there. Or better yet, they will try to suck you into their dark portal or find others just like them to help them keep scratching at the wounds that have grown scabs so that they can stay broken.

Here is a picture of how brokenness should be handled; take a glass and drop it and tell me what your first reaction is. Do you keep walking in the spot with the broken glass? Or do you wipe it up with your bare hands, or do you pause? Majority of us pause and see where the glass has shatter or spread to, then we carefully begin picking up the biggest pieces and are careful to gather the smaller chards of glass so that no one else gets injured by the tiny pieces. No matter how careful some of us are we may end up with a piece of glass in our foot and this can cause a lot of pain and immediately immobilizes you; nonetheless, you approach the broken glass with caution.

Brokenness is hard to repair and no matter how delicately you glue pieces of something broken back together it's never quite the same. Some fractured things such as cups, plates and mirrors cannot be repaired once damaged either. And if you try to handle these broken items without caution you can do more harm to yourself trying to repair them than just discarding them.

This approach should be taken in everyday interactions also. Repairing broken people is a supernatural task. Only a loving Creator can repurpose and completely mend brokenness. When we try to approach and help people still choosing to operate in their trauma, we can end up injured and in need of rescuing.

I used to think that broken people preyed on caring empaths, but after some self-examination, it can also be the other way around. I have always tried to heal others and ended up more injured than when I started. My philanthropist heart believed that I could love someone enough to change. Fifteen years later, I was the one trying to make sense of the fractured remnants of my life. Trying to fix a person that didn't want to change was like trying to swim upstream. I made myself miserable fighting a person for their healing.

People aren't capable of loving you more than they can love themselves. Self-preservation is the first law of the land. And preservation of life supersedes law. This is true in the event that someone is going to take your life, then you have a right to defend your own life. But there are some that believe getting their needs and desires met supersedes the law. Broken people have mastered the art of preserving self. However, it is always at the expense of a willing but very unsuspecting love junkie. You know the person that loves the idea of being in love and if they just tweak the person of their love interest, they will make the perfect person. Or the one that sees good in everyone but hasn't realized yet that you can't want more for a person than they want for themselves. If they haven't seen in themselves what you see in them, you will get stuck doing all the work while they watch. Your hurt feelings are collateral damage and you have to use you to fix brokenness. By the time you find this out you are often left broken, empty and angry.

Broken people will project their unhealed traumas on you and then label you as the weak one or the crazy person. On so many and all levels, taking time to know yourself is one of the main ingredients involved in the making of a better you. Two incomplete people cannot make a whole person. Two fragmented people hooking up does not equal completion. It's more like a jigsaw puzzle. People will come pretending to be whole but are broken distractions wearing duct tape, and the end result is always them leaving with more from you than they deposited into your life.

These people come and eat all of the good fruit that you have produced in your life and won't even spit the seeds back in a napkin for you so that you can replant them to grow good fruit again.

The worst part about broken people is most of them don't know that they are in bad shape until all of their enablers or fixers are removed. It's someone from the outside that has no biases or investments in them, and they come along and shed light on who they are, and they see the same things that others have been confronting them about for years.

People operating in their trauma have gotten so used to breaking things and then trying to replace them that they are shocked when they are addressed about their poor stewardship. You can't replace everything that you break. Some things are one-of-a-kind and can't be purchased or replicated. Meaningful relationships are one of the things that aren't easy to replace. Relationships are rare finds, especially the kind of relationships where some are knit together spiritually. I believe these are once-in-a-lifetime occurrences.

Broken people can only see through the mirror of their own imagination, but real reflections of themselves create anxiety and an overwhelming surge of defensiveness. And the craziest thing is that the only thing the broken one needs to do is humbly admit that they're in the need of help and start the walk in a new direction. The unknown is scary, so people hold on to pride and anger because they think that makes them strong, when really it is causing their brokenness.

As women, we are naturally nurturers by design, and if we love people, we want them to be ok, sometimes even to the point that we risk our own mental, spiritual and physical health. Rough statistics show that 30 percent of caregivers die before the people that they are caring for, mainly because they are busy caring for the ailing person and ignoring their own body signaling that it is failing. Often by the time the women realizes it they are far beyond help or just suddenly drop dead because they didn't even catch the warning signs.

Most of us have flown, and when the flight attendant is giving safety instructions, she says, "In case of loss of pressure the oxygen mask comes down and if you are traveling with small children or are sitting next to an elderly person, remember to put your mask on then proceed to help the person next to you." This concept is also true in life; there are some projects in people that are better off left to the Creator.

"If it is possible, as far as it depends on you live, at peace with everyone." (Romans 12:18)

"Open thy mouth for the dumb in the cause of all such as are appointed to destruction. Open thy mouth, judge righteously, and plead the cause of the poor and needy. Who can find a virtuous woman? For her price is far above rubies." (Proverbs 31:8-10)

We are commanded to live in peace when it is possible, and not to seek vengeance but leave room for the wrath of Yahua.

However, Yeshua advised us that there would always be poor, widows and orphans among us and there is no room for silence when you see your fellow man/woman being oppressed, overlooked or mistreated.

Duet 15:11: "There will always be poor people in the land, therefore I command you to be openhanded toward your fellow Israelites who are poor and needy in your land."

Matt 26:11: "The poor you will always have with you, but you will not always have me.

Seeing the oppressed should move fellow citizens to compassion and in a direction to meet their needs but not at the expense of peace and sanity.

I believe that if I can't help you, I won't hinder you, but others live by the mentality, "If you can't beat them you might as well join them." You can only lead a person who wants to follow. I am trying to stay sane. I encourage others to learn to work with the tools I am equipping them with, not try and kill the person with the tools they are trying to give them. Stop investing in people who are focused on staying in the same predicament and gravitate to those that desire to be made whole.

Lead,   Love   and   Thrive

Pruning Produces Good Fruit

I have had my share of ground zero rebuilds, especially being a business owner, mother, wife, friend and visionary. Some of my investments have went belly up and left me wondering how I would ever recover from the misfortune. I have had dreams shattered and had doors open that I never thought I would be given the keys to.

I've had mutual breakups and then some that caught me completely off guard as well as some that I still can praise dance about being free from.

I've outgrown friends and some aren't vibing on the same frequency that I'm riding and that has become ok too, because we are all on a journey and it isn't about everyone arriving at the same time. Sometimes, some of us have to move out of the way for those that rely too heavily on our presence so that they will to have room to grow.

Some go ahead of others to be the oracle to usher them into the light. With that being said I have had to go through some rigorous grooming in order to be the one to carry the torch. At least that is what has been conveyed to me in my quiet meditation time. My scars aren't all visible but the story of how I got them has been recycled a time or two.

Pruning is a regular part of plant maintenance involving the selective removal of shoots, branches, flowers and buds. Those that aren't familiar with agriculture and why this is done think it's a little harsh once you see what the plant or tree is reduced to, but when you understand why, you can really apply the process to your own life.

And also rest assure that the vinedresser or master gardener knows what to take away and what to leave. Pruning wounds the plant, but plants respond different to wounding than we do.

In plants, damaged areas seal, creating a callused area compartmentalizing the wound and this limits any decay that could occur from the natural death of the branches. Humans' wounds heal and plant wounds seal but the purpose for it is beneficial to the plant and others that will use the plant. It improves the appearance or the health of the plant; for example, it gets rid of disease or insect damaged branches.

Controls the size of the plant so that it remains in better proportion with your landscape. For prevention of personal injury or property damage, corrective pruning also reduces wind resistance in trees. Pruning is done to train your plants to produce stronger and more vigorous trees.

Proper pruning of flowering buds encourages early vegetation growth, stimulates flowering and helps produce larger fruit, in some species of plants.

Last and most important, it is done to rejuvenate old trees and shrubs to make them more attractive and to restore and enhance the beauty of these plants. Humans are intricately designed beings. The brain produces at least twice as many cells than it actually needs to work properly at birth.

As the brain grows and learns to survive in its environments, neural connections that aren't used gradually disappear from the brain as it matures. That's why it's easier to teach an infant more than one language or certain skills should be developed young verses later in life. In psychology, the reduction of neurons, synapses and axons is called the brain's pruning process. If certain experiences, and environments aren't stimulated as a child, you lose certain abilities, theoretically speaking, because we see people with the ability to adapt, learn and change if they are determined to.

In this life, we experience the loss of loved ones, friendships and material items; however, we can only control how we respond to these uncontrolled events. All material items we possess are given to us whether we work and have a job that provides money, or we inherit it. We have been gifted with the ability to think, reason, choose, create, and that which is given to us has a time limit on it, and we don't know how long we will be in possession of it or when we may need to repair or replace items so for the time being we are told to be good stewards of what has been entrusted to us.

We are all on display whether we like to admit it or not and others watch how we handle life when adversity comes our way. We have those that cheer us on and pray for us as we participate in the journey called life and then we have those that chant against us and prey on us hoping that our setbacks and failures will deal us the coup de grâce. The only way you won't reach your designated end will be to keep operating in disorder and disobedience. When a person continues to manifest the same behaviors repeatedly, believe the behavior. So, don't be ashamed and definitely don't stay too long in your despair when it seems your branches have been clipped and others are eyeing you. Remember, you are cut back to produce, grow and be replenished, because the same ones that wouldn't even sprinkle water on you to help you survive will need the shade, shelter, fruit and life that you will give off after this process.

Ever see a large beautiful tree fallen in the wilderness with its roots detached? This tree looked perfectly healthy amongst the other trees. Same height as the other trees with long branches and green leaves appearing to be the stronger and most beautiful amongst the other trees. But something went terribly wrong; the storm winds blew, and the rain poured down. The other trees whose root systems were stronger descended deeper into the foundation of the soil they were planted in. But the tree that fell lacked the ability to sink its roots deeper into the soil, so the storm uprooted the tree headlong. A few things played a role in this happening. The tree was planted poorly from the beginning, it wasn't planted in the right place or it was over crowded and the roots didn't get enough nutrients.

See, when the other trees sustained injury, they held on tighter to their foundation, the cutting back of the branches or fallen branches may have made the tree look funny for a season. Sometimes the storm would make the injured trees appear to others as bare and fruitless. But deep beneath the surface, the roots of the other trees were being forced to reach deeper underground and spread out further. It has been said that some trees' roots can spread more than 50 feet. Pruning a tree while the tree is young helps to ensure strong tree structure. Pruning causes the tree to become more stable than before the pruning.

I have often observed people and because of their appearance and position many believed that they have it all together. You know they look the part, adorn themselves with the right clothes and even mingle in the right circles, but all aren't what they appear to be. Circumstances of life occur, and they are uprooted and stumbling. Leaving those that were watching them to question, "What happened?" It looked like they were standing just as regal and strong as all the others in their circle, but their foundation wasn't one that could sustain adversity.

Stop minimizing who you are and what you are capable of because of appearances of those around you. Adversity and injury may be a component of the making of you, but it doesn't make what you bring to the table less significant.

Quit muting your song because you are worried about what others might say. How much more beautiful would some women be if they operated in their own gifts, talents and abilities? What if we quit measuring ourselves up against other women who are really broken? So many broken women are trying to lead as they cover up their unhealed wounds. I have witnessed many unhealed women that use soapboxes to propagate agendas that they are too traumatized to heal from themselves. So, they operate not being transparent and manipulate the order of operation and find themselves more damaged than when they started. They teach other broken women to plant seeds of disorder because they became bitter and resistant in their season of pruning. And missed the opportunity to bear nourishing fruit that tastes good to the palate and heals the mind, body and soul. Being cut down has allowed me to be strong and exercise the power of overcoming the seasons designed to grow me. I can covey to you now that the pruning I was allowed to experience was filtered through the divine will of a gentle and nurturing creator. I realize it is the responsibility of a woman whose basket is full of a ripe harvest to feed those that desire nourishment.

Reciprocity is the Greatest Love Song

"For the Yahua ELOHIM is a sun and shield: Yahua will give grace and glory: no good thing will he withhold from them that walk uprightly."

(Psalm 84:11)

The statement, "Your vibe attracts your tribe," is so true. People usually pull in the same direction of those who share the same values, temperaments and dispositions as themselves. And then you have people who act as parasites who can feel the frequency of a giver a mile away and will gravitate to you. These people always come with a poor-me story and the everyone-does-them-so-wrong song. They play the game long enough to suck you into their portal and you will spend more time trying to get out of there dark hole than you will enjoy being in their presence.

I have learned some hard and costly lessons because I wanted to see others win. To see a person win involves choosing a winner, one with love of their Creator and love for self is insurmountable. I always believed that you get what you give. This wasn't true dealing with takers. The more I

180

invested the more they took. I had to stop giving and set some firm boundaries or else my cup was going to end up empty.

Cheering for a person to win isn't wrong, it's wrong when the people you invest in are only for themselves, and the only investment they are willing to make is the one that consists of words and no deeds.

We have the tendency to believe the things we hear and not wait for the actions of the words to manifest the truth.

Have you ever wondered what causes a person to take and not give anything back? I have often been the puzzled one left wondering how a person takes and doesn't give. Especially when I give generously and with love. Love is a deliberate act and the universe mimics this precept. The loyal person or, in a biblical sense, a righteous person has no place in the life of an unrighteous person. A righteous person is a giver and operates the way Yahua has designed the universe to operate; give and take. So, a giver is only good for a taker but never for the whole universe. The universe is supposed to prosper from the gifts that the creator has endowed the giver with but when a taker intercepts a gift they don't want anyone to benefit from the giver because all the taker knows how to do is devour and they will manipulate, lie and go as far as cry to distract and prolong your stay in their death grip. A person

181

whose heart hasn't been primed in truth and the soil of their life lacks no nourishment for the seeds a righteous person will bring and try to plant there.

Living out loud is more than being a carbon copy!

Being whole is true beauty; transparency is key!

Your Fight is the Light That Makes You Shine

"But he knowth the way that I take; when he hath tried me, I
shall come forth as gold."

(Job 23:10)

A picture is worth a thousand words. Pictures can
capture a moment in time but only the people present for the
capturing of the picture can give the narrative of the story
about how the picture came to be. Some of the most beautiful
people I know have experienced the most ugly that life has to
offer. The thing that makes them beautiful is that they allowed
the pain to refine them and not restrain them. Life is filled
with trials and transitions and it's not about how you start but
how you finish. "Life is truly 10 percent of what happens to
you and 90 percent how you react to it." –Charles R. Swindol

The premise for this book, *Beauty from Brokenness* are
lessons from events that I thought would kill me. I am not
perfect and know that complete perfection only comes once I
have transcended from this flawed dimension into the infinite.
I decided early in my journey to never let disappointments,
embarrassments or epic failure prevent me from pressing

forward toward the mark. I adopted the what-doesn't-kill-me-will-make-me-stronger approach and have revised it a time or two. I am intentional when it comes to never letting my "good be spoken evil of" I own the paths I have chosen, especially the ones I had to be rescued from. And I play the cards from the hand life has dealt me. As I write today, I can testify that, "All things do work together for good for those that love Yah and are called according to his purpose." (Romans 8:28)

You don't get a second chance to make a first impression. And the same is true about life; you don't get a second chance to do life in this realm over. Since I am only a vessel and the contents inside of the vessel can only be used if its poured out, I have chosen to be willing. The word states that we that obey Yah and take him at his word are vessels of light. If we take the light and hide it, what use is it to others? But if we allow the light to be placed on display, it can light up the world. Your cracked vessel has something to reveal.

Embrace being unapologetic about choosing to live in truth, with integrity and last of all with no regrets. Leave fear out of your equation, because fear usually involves the opinions you think others will have of you. Most of their opinions are birthed and nurtured by their own fears and failures. People will talk about you dead or alive, make sure of the fact that when they do talk about you, they tell the real truth not a colorful lie. Tell your story if it will edify and help someone struggling to embrace their path.

Secrets and concealing are coupled with guilt and torment. Secrets have no power once they are exposed. Repent, move forward, repeat! No man or woman should have leverage over you to hold you hostage by darkness. Be the administration of you and your narrative guided by obedience and truth.

When you sit around other women, make sure your conversation facilitates them on a treasure hunt to find where you got your pearls of wisdom from. Don't dine in the company of those that eat plates of regurgitated nonsense. Nutrients that cultivate a "Glow Up" comes from feasting on things that produce life. "For the word of God is alive and active. Sharper than any double-edged sword, it penetrates even to dividing soul and spirit, joints and marrow; it judges the thoughts and attitudes of the heart." (Hebrews 4:12)

Remember, beauty is more than just the exterior, some people wear beautiful things and have fair appearances but lack true substance. Adorning the outside of your physical body but parading around with an injured soul is a travesty.

No matter what you try to hide the injury with, it will expose itself eventually. They are only costumes that people wear a lot of times to hide the real fiasco that exists underneath their embellished physique.

There's a lot more than meets the eye when it comes to what things look like and what they really are. Don't dumb it down because others can't stand in the spotlight that your Creator has put on you, when the spotlight is on you, I encourage you leave all you got to give on the stage because you can't take it with you.

Lastly, remember that pressure makes diamonds; the more pressure that you have overcome the more brilliant the shine.   Fight   on.

Transparency

"People have a greater respect for you evolving into a butterfly when you are truthful about once being a caterpillar."

~Nia Marie

I can remember the first time I participated in a biblical-based women's workshop and the table that I was sitting at was a table filled with women that I was acquainted with, meaning we all had attended the same congregation but never really got a chance to get connected on a more intimate level until this event. While fellowshipping and sharing some obstacles that I've encountered and overcome, one of the ladies finally stated to me, "I've always looked at you and I just figured you were born with a silver spoon in your mouth and always had what you have handed to you." Funny right? But this is why a lot of us (women/men) don't connect or get free from the lies the mirrors tell, the lies they believed from the enemy and the story we write about others before we have ever even gotten a chance to break bread with them.

Secrets have no power once they are exposed. The unknown will paralyze you if you don't have the courage to move forward. Coming out of darkness for some is rewarding and breathtaking and for others it is blinding because they can't handle the light that permeates at the end of the tunnel.

Light has the potential to expose the things that we have saved tucked away in the darkness not trying to see. So, instead of allowing the light to shine through and grow, a lot of people have elected to dwell in the darkness with others that are running from exposure.

Most choose to do so because they have all mastered the same old song and they play it on repeat and have become hypnotized by its tune that tells them they are okay where they are. Anyone who has ever done a science project about what grows in stagnant, damp, wet areas knows that eventually darkness produces mold, stench and creeping things that can make you very sick.

No man or woman should have leverage over you to hold you hostage by darkness. The ability to make choices and mistakes and deal with the fallout is a sign of strength. Fresh eyes can give greater objectivity.

Doctrine, friends and leadership of certain organizations can help keep you in bondage or in a cocoon long after you have developed your wings to fly. Because of the fact that slavery and the way scripture has been wrongly conveyed, we allow leadership and tradition to allow others to mistreat devour and demean us. I have nursed dead situations longer than they should have been and ending up almost falling into a cycle of depression and anger. Depression, because I was doing what I was told was right according to doctrine. And anger because I found out that the formula for making a marriage work was a lie. Truth had been manipulated. Manipulated by ignorance, and people who had subscribed to a way of teaching that didn't have a clear understanding of what marriage was. I trusted them without doing my own investing in studying the doctrine I said I believed. The whole universe was created with intent and purpose.

As humans, we will try to cope and preserve ourselves and life at all costs. I had subscribed to applying affirmations from and investing love where it was being served back to me cold and in stingy rations. Until one day I stopped listening to words and paid attention to how functional the situation I was in worked. It looked like it worked for the others from the outside looking in but pretending doesn't work for me, it made me miserable. I often felt like I was under water drowning. I stayed because I believed this made me strong, that because I could keep functioning and navigating through hurt, shame and disappointment I would be blessed for staying in a dysfunctional marriage because marriage was "God" ordained. I was trying to speak life into my situation while also trying to maintain my sanity because I knew the situation would never work because all of the offenses that were taking place. Most of them were against everything my DNA was comprised of. I was close to committing murder and mayhem while trying to stay in a vicious cycle. This is the definition of insanity and was a major obstruction to my peace. I had two choices: stay and be miserable or leave and evolve into the woman that I know I was created to be.

People will call you strong when you endure abuse, cheating, and embarrassment, but the truth about this reality is it's not strength, you just have a high pain tolerance and the constant pain has rendered you weak and the only thing that makes sense is to handle the most important things in life and those are bare necessities. I don't like bare necessity living; I like exceptional, abundant more than enough living. I wanted overflow living so that I have enough love, joy, and peace for those whose paths that I would cross living.

And spectators think you are invincible, when in all actuality you have just shut down to preserve your mental health and your lifeforce. If some of us would have continued to try and fight some battles on empty, we would be on skid row pushing baskets and talking to inanimate objects.

Self-preservation is a must until we muster up enough strength to run. Strong isn't staying, you gain real velocity when you walk away from that which is holding you captive and weighing you down.

Strength is moving forward unaware of what is on the other side of the mountain.

Appearances aren't everything, behind many beautiful eyes and faces are stories that can make your life look like a cakewalk.

There's a lot more than meets the eye when it comes to what things look like. A picture doesn't reveal what's really going on, it's just a snapshot of one particular moment in time that is eternally captured for others to admire, view or see from the vantage point they choose to see you in.

Know When to Walk Away

"You've got to learn to leave the table when love's no longer being served."

~Nina Simone

"You are going to miss out if you move on," or "Your loss, your choice," were a couple of statements that kept me stuck in an insane cycle longer than I should have stayed. This was the speech of a person who didn't have the power to change from a direction that was headed nowhere fast, they lacked the courage to admit that they didn't know how to change. This person knew that what he had his hooks sunk into was the best thing he had ever encountered and with each indiscretion he was losing his grip. In all actuality, their statement is true in an ironic way! See, once I decided to move on from them, I was able to miss all of the disappointments, heartache and damage that he kept multiplying in my life. I quit missing out on the true blessings that were waiting for me. Once I walked away from what was distracting me, doors began to open, and anxiety and heavy loads were lifted.

A writer that I haven't heard of until recently and decided to purge myself with words is James Baldwin and one of his quotes spoke resolve to my soul and it was, "I don't believe what you say because I see what you do!"

When a person has proven to you with their actions over and over again that they lack the capacity to pay up on their promises, believe them. The one you are holding on to is merely a shallow, stagnant pond of other people's stuff that they have collected along the way. Then they sell it back to you because you are good at making beautiful things out of other people's messes but can never make good on the things that they promise to give you.

The taker lives in a constant state of slavery because for everything they take, they have to render it back sevenfold and instead of contribution, they stay looking for a source of energy to draw from because without one they eventually will cease to exist. So, they live on this perpetual cycle of trying to convince vulnerable people, or people unaware of their worth that they are only made better because they are in their lives, when in all actuality, they are slowing down the persons momentum with the baggage that they so need to dump on someone else, so that they look better than the person they really can't live without.

I have seen so many beautiful people destroyed by distractions that have come in the form of a man serving fake love. Some have come in the form of a man that seems to have the missing puzzle piece to what you thought you couldn't live without only later to reveal that he was sent by Hasatan himself. You have whispered prayers for love to only have them intercepted by the enemy in the vicinity when your heart's desire was being spoken. Some distractions can come in the form of fake friends and askholes. This person is one who likes to hear what motivates you and pretends that they are seeking council only to waste your time with the same shit they have been troubled with for the last 20 years and have no intention of doing anything you tell them different. They just want a pep talk but will continue to doubt themselves and believe the lie that they tell themselves. I learned to save my words for someone willing to evolve.

Walking away helped me to walk in the newness of the beauty I neglected to own. The one I always had but was always adorning the people I needed to remove my presence from.

I have learned to escaped being an accessory for another person's happiness. Making them shine while they tarnish my glow. I have lived miserably while they have shined, I have learned if a man doesn't come with something to give you that will make you a better woman, he is coming to take or to be built up while he tears you down.

If it's one thing that life has taught me is the true meaning of what casting your pearls before swine means. When I was tired of picking up trampled pearls I exited gracefully. Matt 7:6: "Give not that is what is holy unto the dogs, neither cast ye your pearls before swine, lest they trample them under their feet, and turn again and rend you."

The lies that were used to entrap me was that "things would change" and I had meditated on the quote, "I was going to miss out," that I almost believed it. I believed someone else would benefit from all that I had invested in the relationship. I used to worry that another would prosper from years I invested. I learned that couldn't be farther from the truth, because the truth was that a taker will never have enough to prosper. They are always in debt. They can only be as complete and full as you make them. Running on empty is who they are when they come, and they leave full once they have depleted you. They hope that will hold them over until they meet the next "source." When the new victim wasn't feeling his cup was full enough, he would throw out enough bait to reel me in to keep me investing sincere love while he sold me and whoever else would believe him a dream. I will add that I never believed a lie that I didn't want to be true! There was nothing wrong with my desire for love, but this person had already showed me more times than I could count that love wasn't their strong suit. So, all along, the situation worked because I was the one who wanted it to work. You can't scam a person unless they are willing to participate. I take full responsibility for allowing the people I did to continue to give me less than I deserved.

I stand guilty in the area of loving the wrong people longer; too long and investing too much with no return. It wasn't until the relationship was over that I look back and wonder how did I allow myself to even get that emotionally invested? I had been buying and paying for the lie with my own blood, sweat and tears. No matter what I felt, the person owed me for the love I invested. I owed myself more and I jumped off the hamster wheel. For 12 years I had it in mind that this person owed me for all that I had invested in this relationship. But the longer I waited for reparations the more I grew tired and angry. I was beating a dead horse; the person didn't possess the power to return anything I had given. And a person can't give you what they don't have. They can only give you what is in their heart and in their case, it was a lot of folly, deceit and secrets. I was the source that sustained us both until I finally grew exhausted. The universe is designed to give and receive never take and not give back. When a person can't love you as they love themselves, it's time to walk away. There is a love that doesn't involve suffering first to prove that you are worthy, and that's the love I have subscribed to. I pray you join me.

My Auntie Marcia always has nuggets of wisdom when she calls me or when we interact. She always leaves the conversation with something for me to meditate on. Before we hung up from one of our conversations, she said, "Remember the gladiator?"

I said, "Yes."

She said, "He entered the arena, fought and was victorious, but he exited dead." Her charge to me was, "Stop engaging with everyone and learn how to exit!" Powerful, right? Watch who you engage with and pay attention to how people arrive to the place in life that they are in.

Know your opponent!

Do You Know Who You Are?

"Before I formed thee in the belly I knew you; and before you came forth out of the womb I sanctified thee, and I Ordained the a prophet unto the nations."

(Jer. 1:5)

This particular scripture stated Yah was speaking to the prophet Jeremiah. Jeremiah had been chosen to speak to the nation of Israel about impending judgment for falling away from Yah. They had begun to act like the nations that Yah had allowed Israel to conquer before coming into the promised land. Jeremiah was not confident in his message being received nor did he believe he was mature enough to convey the words of Yahua. Yah told him to not be afraid of the countenance of their faces because He was with him. Yah touched his mouth with his hand and told him he had put his words in Jeremiah's mouth.

We are all known and have a mission to accomplish while we are here. Before Yah gives us a task to complete, He equips us and reminds us of who we are in Him.

Oblivious and unaware people very seldom make a wave or shake anything up. It is usually a person who has become aware of their purpose and destiny that will become the catalyst that will change the course of destiny. This is when people that have grown accustom to you being just oblivious and acquiescing to the script and behaviors of everyday life will say you are tripping, or you have changed.

No man or woman who hasn't owned their own truth about where they come from and who they are can tell me who I am! Change can really frighten some people.

The most frustrating and liberating experience in life is looking for acceptance and others trying to tell you who and how to be when you have already discovered that you are. All men and women are created equal, if I may? But not all will embrace who they are.

We are all equal as far as having human rights but designed different and for different purposes. When you realize how much power is harvested when you realize who you are, you will straighten your back and walk with shoulders back and head held high.

Introspective and being able to look into the mirror with honest eyes are the key to being who you were designed to be. Accepting your fears, weaknesses and failures and presenting them to Yah so that he can give you beauty for your ashes.

I used to think I knew myself and had it all figured out until I kept repeating the same disappointments over and over and I finally had to take a step back and look at the situations I kept gravitating to and why. I had to allow some layers of tough skin I had grown to be peeled back. The Most High revealed a very intricate chapter to my story and that is you don't know who you are until you have been completely broken and I am your source. Low points are where I learned humility and dependence on Yah. It was once told by a really good friend and at the time a sounding board and advisor while I was experiencing an unexpected loss. What he mentioned to me has stayed although it has taken me until now to realize what he was conveying to me.

He said, "In order for you to understand who you are, you have to understand your mother's heart and try to embrace who she is."

Well, I thought, this is going to be hard! Because my mother was born and raised in the era where everything was a secret and you didn't dare ever tell your children that you weren't perfect or ever made mistakes. And plus, my relationship with her is very strained. Not because she wasn't a mother that wasn't around but because she and I fought every step of the way during my childhood and adolescences. In my teenage years, incidents occurred, and she didn't protect me as I believe a mother should, so that fractured our relationship more. Because of the lack of protection, I became my own advocate and was emancipated by the age of 16. I was a visionary, creative and unapologetic about the choices that I made. As I progressed into my adult life, we didn't work on the necessary repairs of the fractured relationship either. She spent most of the time operating in avoidance of any discussion about my offenses toward her. She didn't understand or embrace the beauty of having a free spirit for a child. She interpreted me exploring and always being different as me hating her.

She was controlling because she was raised by strong-willed controlling women and she never embraced change because it disrupted her norm. She never allowed herself, as an adult, the liberty to find an identity of her own. She saw me as opposing her because I knew what I wanted without being told that I should like this and settle for that. It became a pattern of first she would try and force her will upon me to the point that it would become physical. I eventually left home at 13 after deciding I wasn't going to be physically reprimanded. Especially by the person who didn't protect me when I needed her most. I wasn't a disobedient disrespectful child, I just always had a fire burning inside that told me I could be more and do more, it was just never nurtured at home.

So, I looked for validation from the wrong sources. I subjected myself to being mistreated at the hands of boys who claimed to love me and I learned some hard lessons about what love was and wasn't. It was later in life that my mother told me that she admired me because I was strong and a fighter and that's why she didn't hug or nurture me because she didn't think I needed it. And she wished she had fostered some of the friendships and relationships I had. She failed to realize that she had the first crack at loving, nurturing and shaping me. But in parenting, there is such a small window of opportunity to make positive lasting impressions in your children's lives. She didn't learn to watch and cultivate what was in her oldest child. What we, as parents, deposit early on in our children will later render the blessings from our investments. Understand that my sharing is in no attempt a way to try and dishonor my mother, she has her own cross to bear and I believe that if she ever told her story she could be healed from a lot of her regrets. I am being transparent because I have chosen wholeness and healing. I have realized that I am my mother and I have chosen to feed the qualities that I have inherited and use the mistakes and choices that haven't rendered positive outcomes as a template for my life to become complete.

Long story short, we cannot identify certain behaviors in others unless we possess them ourselves. And in learning who I am, I understood a lot more of why she is who she is. She is strong-willed and determined, however, it has been to her detriment. I am passionate and loving and want to see others win. She wants what others have and only for herself, so lacking the ability to love and release a person to grow and share what is in abundance has caused her to lack. When I say lack I mean in joy, love and companionship.

Learning is observational and a lot of who we are lies in who we have emerged from. I have had to stop being angry and resenting certain things that I didn't understand about my mother while I was coming into my own. I swore I would be nothing like her when in all actuality I have inherited a portion of my mother's soul. The things that I thought made her weak have been my strengths and equipped me with the ability to build upon and share.

I have chosen to give my daughters a legacy of my arrival so that in my departure they don't feel like they are lost as I often do with my mother. Her inability to purge and share has trapped her in a state of anguish and guilt, because I am me, because of her and in spite of what I choose not to repeat.

Identity is everything and understanding why you are who you are is imperative to creating whole and complete individuals.

Don't hide or remove the ancient markers; however, point to the path that leads to understanding and a wholesome life.

Take the good and dispose of the bad to become complete. I was taught growing up that children don't come with instructions, later to find out that statement was a regurgitated lie! Life as well as children come with loving instructions from our Creator, people just skip reading the instructions.

Torah is the antidote for identity crises; read, obey and walk in the newness of who you are.

Proverbs 22:6 states: "Raise a child in the way that they should and when they are old, they will not depart from the path."

Ephesians 6:4 says, "Parents don't exasperate or provoke your children, instead bring them up in the training and instruction of Yahua."

We spend so much time trying to put components into our children that only decorate the outside or create habits and traditions that don't please the father when he designed us with a vacuum in our souls that begins searching for our creator the moment we are self-aware.

Stop Wearing Jackets That Don't Fit Anymore

"Wherefore if any man is in Hamasciach, he is a new creature: the old things are passed away; behold, they are become new."

(2 Corinthians 5:17)

"As a man thinks so he becomes" Proverbs 23:7 Some people ruminate on their pain so long that they make the abuse, disregard, lies and pain that was inflicted on them by others fit them like a tailored suit.

After constructing the outfit, they embrace it and wear it. They become a victim to a jacket that never fit and they either shrink it to fit or they squeeze into it and allow it to constrict their life like a straitjacket at an asylum.

If we continue living, physically aging is inevitable, but growing up is optional.

We should always strive toward elevation; elevating helps you to see things clearer and from a different vantage point. Purpose in this life is to never stay the same if the nature of our existence isn't beneficial. As your travel through life's peaks and valleys, you will need to leave some mindsets, acquaintances, and friends behind. This doesn't mean you don't love them or that you hate them. It just means that everyone won't come with you into all the seasons of your journey in life. You have committed lifetime friends, casual friends and those that you will outgrow.

A principle I adopted at 18 was to set five-year goals and write them down. Writing commits thoughts and words to your memory. When you see things, they become real to you and then you can make the necessary adjustments to see your thoughts and words manifest into reality. Thoughts and words carry power they possess the power to build up or tear down, to heal or destroy.

Living should be done intentionally and with purpose. Continuing to try to live up to personas and things that are in the past will stop your progression and propel you into a downward spiral of chasing the past. Thoughts and words are powerful, allowing others to speak into our lives can be detrimental if they aren't speaking words of life and truth. Just like viruses are airborne and infections are contracted by coming into close contact with the carrier or from touching, ingesting or wearing something an infected person has worn; such is it with what is commanded over your life. Especially by people that are negative and directionless.

In ancient times, things that could infect and spread and contaminate others was rid of by fire, yes fire has cleansing properties. It can consume something that you don't want to leave any evidence of, or it can purify and leave precious metals and stones brilliantly shining.

You see they give you images of others that you see as having it all but really, they are living a scripted life, a life that is controlled by what will keep people coming back to buying jackets that don't fit. There are so many broken children living in adult bodies mimicking adult lives. I have encountered adults who still have not been able to move past being a 10-year-old paralyzed because of fear of failure or rejection. Some people will even digress to unfavorable events to put back on old jackets because they are more comfortable in those jackets than ones that fit.

Then some will do anything, even if it is destructive. Just to be recognized they will fight, claw and kill to leave their mark and make a name for themselves. That mentality and way of thinking has kept us in a perpetual state of emergency.

And you can see the residual evidence of it. Men and women living up to the stereotypes seen on television and media, Shows like *Blackish* with truths hidden in plain sight

212

about how "others" see us. The having babies by five and six different women and calling themselves pimps and solid niggas, women boosting and teaching their children to use their looks and body to get necessities instead of teaching them that wise women build, and real men cover and protect and provide for their families and make real commitments and that your word is your bond. And a name holds weight and when your name is spoken of, make sure it isn't something that will not bring shame upon generations to come.

The thing that you believe and obey becomes your master, so we have designers, performers and scripts written and we hold to them as if they are the gospel, meanwhile rejecting what is real.

"The adversary comes to accuse, steal, kill, and destroy but remember what the most high did for the priest Joshua in the book of Zechariah when it was time for him to minister? He gave him a new robe! Stop wearing jackets that don't fit and walk into your new ministry with a jacket that fits you." (Zechariah 3:1-5)

Remember to Love Yourself

I am a self-professed philanthropist that loves hard, long, and am loyal to a fault. I have often selflessly loved and overlooked my own needs and desires to encourage and invest in others. After allowing others to render me bankrupt emotionally and physically and put me in a strained financial position, I have come to an epiphany. I am tired of being the only loyal one in relationships.

I had to realize that people will take all that you have to give and then won't deposit an ounce of the love back of what you have given them. If you don't love yourself, people will treat you with the same regard. It's almost like two sisters that publicly fight and bicker with each other and publicly attack each other, they have no united front. When others are allowed to see this behavior, they don't have a problem attacking the sister because they see the lack of esteem, they have for one another so it shouldn't be a problem to add some damage also.

Self-love and confidence are more attractive than any feature one can possess.

Self-love speaks volumes and you can feel it when a person enters a room; it gives off a sweet fragrance that causes people to pay attention to the person that enters the building. A person that has embraced themselves has a presences that makes others want to know their story; what is the force that drives them? What have they endured? What obstacles have they overcome? And lastly, how can I get some of that? The way we live and overcome challenges should always reference people in a direction to see the creator and how much he loves us first.

Not in a narcissistic self-absorbed way but the love and the knowledge of the fact that you are fearfully and wonderfully designed with your own predestined qualities to contribute to the universe and knowing that you are an authentic design like a fingerprint, no two are identical. And to know that you are known by the one whom designed you and having a personal relationship with your Creator is enough to be confident in. Knowing that as much as you can walk on hot coals and heal from the burns, you deserve to be treated like family heirloom china: delicate and priceless. This kind of self-love commands attention and loving yourself involves a huge amount of knowing what you deserve and shouldn't tolerate.

I have learned that just because I can endure or withstand something doesn't mean I should subject myself to it or even allow certain people or places to be graced with my presence, because repairing your emotions and mind takes time. Time is valuable, more like priceless, and you can't get any of the time wasted back. You can learn a lesson at the expense of blemished character and bruised emotions. And the question is why would you do that when you have people like me to show you a more excellent and effective way?

Yes, I have heard people appreciate a lesson that they purchased. It is appreciated far more than a free one because they sacrificed to receive it, but most bought lessons are cruel. Consider this book a costly lesson and apply the principles from my colorful journey of bumps and bruises to avoid heartache of your own.

I stated earlier that a person that loves themselves knows what love is and what kind of love they deserve. This means we aren't looking to pick up strays that want to take advantage of their love but are waiting on a complete companion to connect with so that the missing component to their equation can balance out.

When the deeds don't match the words that's what you should believe. I have a saying that is sad but true: "People will stress you out and kill you with their madness and even eat the chicken at your funeral and then will be looking for the next person they can kill."

Takers never have enough because their hands stay full from taking everyone else's things and never have their hands open long enough to receive what could possibly be for them. What is meant for you is for you, and if you try to bless someone's life with what they aren't ready for, you participate in the principle of casting pearls before swine to have them trampled upon. Love you and attract another that will do the same.

My prayer on my journey of loving myself is: "Abba (Hebrew for my father) You being perfect and only giving good gifts send me the love that is designed to heal me, restore me, and make me whole. I want to experience real unadulterated love a love only you can provide me with. Amen."

Love is More Than a Word

Stop entertaining people that refuse to celebrate you when you are deserving of it. The Holy manuscript tells us that our Creator rejoices over us.

"The Lord your God is with you, the Mighty Warrior who saves. He will take great delight in you; in his love he will no longer rebuke you, but will rejoice over you with singing."
(Zepahniah 3:17)

When you are in right standing with Him, He will not only rejoice over you but He also will go to war for you! That is the type of father, friend and lover we should embrace. I used to feel like the character Ms. Sophia in *The Color Purple*... "All my life I had to fight!" Not feeling like I had an advocate. Someone who would go to war for me rather good, bad or indifferent that they loved and believed I was worthy of fighting for.

Man! When you think about this every day, we are commanded by the Most High to observe creation and glory in the magnificent hand of the Creator.

Love is free but it is also a choice. Love should be given freely without any expectations other than respect or gratitude shown toward the giver. I mean, love is really free and at the same time it's priceless. You can't put a dollar amount on love. "Greater love has no man than he would lay down his life for a friend." (John 15:13)

Friendship is a covenant relationship or agreement to adhere to certain guidelines and codes and if the relationship lacks boundaries and guidelines, 90% of the time it's a recipe for disaster, and misunderstandings. Love without trust is just a situation! Let's stop subscribing to situations and endorse the true function of love. Western culture has taught us that intimacy is only sex, but to be intimate means to know a person too and enter into a covenant relationship with them. In a relationship, your duty should involve protecting and guarding your family and even laying aside your agenda to see the person you say you love be able to excel to their highest capacity.

If or when those things are violated, then the relationship ceases or is strained, that means everyone should be measured by the honor system. I trust you based on how trustworthy you prove yourself to be, and not by words but by deeds, deeds don't lie. We might say what we don't mean but 99.9% of the time we don't do what we don't mean.

I often wonder where I would be right now or how much money I would have saved by now if I invested in my dreams, desires and potential, instead of seeing more potential in others than they see in themselves. Oh, how content and happy I would be if I loved on myself as hard as I have loved some people who never deserved my kind of love or didn't know how to reciprocate the love back in return. I have learned that people nurtured in love hold a different set of values than those that were raised in environments where they had to just survive.

When seasons of "love" are up, some say leaving is the hardest thing to do when you are in love and it's just not working out, but it is staying where love isn't really love that is a humdinger. Everyone wants to see a return on their investment whether they will admit it or not. Parents want to see their children be successful in school, sports and society after they have invested the correct amount of love, discipline and resources. People open businesses to reap a profit after years of operating not knowing that sometimes the business has to go through some hardships and hard mistakes to render a full profit. And some ventures we have to just cut our losses with.

Relationships are the same way. When love becomes only a word spoken and no action shown, it's a sham. Loving and learning is an investment! "You will know a tree by its fruits!" (Matt. 15-20) deeds don't lie.

No One Can Do You Like You Can Do You

"If you want something done right do it yourself"

~Charles Guillaume Étienne

Have you ever been given a desire that burns so deep in your heart that you know it was divinely sent? Your story is only yours to tell, if you don't tell it, someone else will try and give their watered down rendition of the truth only you know. Or the warped perception based on their biases or prejudices of the vantage point they have been given to see you or your experience.

I have a disclaimer that I mean very seriously, and I tell it to my closest friends, although most people that I allow in my circle live by this unspoken G code.

Don't defend me to others because in your doing so you can reveal things to them that aren't for them to know about me, or you fill in the blanks to a twisted script about me that they are writing, and others will believe it's true because you have been made privy to my inner circle. No one knows the passion, pain, tears and the inflections in your voice or the reason why they are even there. Only the person who has lived through the same adversity and pains can relate.

I was graced with the presence of a beautiful spirit who came in the form of a client. She was such a blessing to me, and our meetings happened about every two to three weeks and the time we spent together while she was at the salon with me was priceless. On the days of her appointment we shared some raw and candid moments as well as some triumphs and tears together. These things only happen when people are being true to who they were designed to be.

I can still hear her telling me this; she said, "You have gifts and blessings that are just waiting on you to pick them up that's all you have to do." She said, "Imagine this journey called life this way: at the end you get to look back and see all of the flowers you left unpicked because you didn't trust the voice inside of you telling you to stop and pick them." She said, "Wouldn't you rather have your bouquet of roses in your basket or look back and see all the ones you left behind?" She was always encouraging me to do the things that were placed in my heart to do and not wait or procrastinate when the desire was placed in my spirit.

The only thing is that if you don't do what has been placed in your heart to do, someone else will do it and you will have to stand on the sidelines and watch them do what you were given charge to do. And the reason for their success won't be because of their ability to do what was shown to you was greater, but their availability and obedience to proceed with just what they had; a vision and a call. And they took the first step of faith and that is done one step at a time. The rest of the story can never be revealed until you obey the first truth. That only you can be who you were created to be. Other people may have the same idea or even be doing the same thing that you have been given a vision to complete, but they aren't going to draw who you were designed to draw.

I have lived long enough and been given enough discernment to know that genuine people don't come a dime a dozen and real people vibe with real people. So, my background, upbringing and environment created the me that only certain people looking for my authenticity will gravitate to and so is the same with you. I have learned that every generation has leaders and not all of them are good. People are always looking to connect and for a place to belong and some don't know that they are being herded by shepherds in wolves' clothing.

My worst quality, and the thing that has sabotaged many of my great calls, is the need to be perfect and waiting for the right time... the right time is now. Now is a powerful position. You don't get a second chance to be in the now if you don't seize the moment. That place in time is unobtainable. I have seen potential and wanted more for people than they want for themselves and taking them on as a personal project only to be robbed of love, time and resources.

Robbed because a robber comes wearing a mask and gets close enough to you to snatch your goods. A thief comes when you aren't expecting him, they calculate and wait until you're not home. A robber has to get physically close enough to snatch what you have. Don't ignore the signs when they are revealed to you about people and their character.

Pray about whom it is you invest in and this is a lot of where I was told to put these principles on paper. Now your investments will be reciprocated because those that want to know what the making of you is, have to make a small investment for your willingness to pour out.

I am a vessel that has been broken to perfection meaning, I know that the Most High has filtered the storms that have broken me through his grace. I am complete enough to be stable in my thoughts and conveying my truth to you but, I have been broken enough to pour the contents within me out to encourage others. I am unapologetic and unashamed of where my Creator has saw fit to bring me from. I am a new creation and refuse to walk in the shadows of what used to be. I have primed my mind with the truth of what Yah says is true and that is there is liberty in the truth of his word. (paraphrased 2 Corinthians 3:17)

Earlier, I made it a point to tell you to not wear the jackets that don't fit anymore because people will try to dress you in a dead person's clothes. Meaning, the people love to dig in the mud of yesteryear. People will reenact old scenarios and recall their very own rendition of an old you, but it will be a Frankenstein monster, they will even try and make you recall things that have long been put to rest and rightfully so. You can't be all that you can be under the direction of people who won't even walk in their own purpose. People may remember the old you but won't take the time to be introduced to who you are becoming. I'm here to tell you it's ok to break some of those people's plates that you have allowed to have a seat at your table! Some People you allowed at your table were never really fit to dine there so make room for the ones Yah will bring your way.

There is someone somewhere suffering in silence or afraid to become who they are already destined to be because of your unwillingness to be transparent and convey your truth

226

only the way that you can. I have tried to cover and protect other's ugly behavior that helped produce the making of me, but it caused me to miss many opportunities. So often there were others that had been watching me dealing with the same issues. They stayed longer in a rut waiting on me to embrace who I was so that they would gain the courage to do the same. Embrace the unique beauty of self and walk in purpose.

Yahua is so right on time with his timing that even as I am penning these words, he is assuring me that only those whom this chapter is for will get this principle.

I believe in divine appointments and I know that one has been set for you, whomever you are. If you are reading this chapter right now my prayer is for you to see the light that is at the end of the dark tunnel of your adversity. When you overcome your adversity, remember to be the light that leads another out to a functional end once you have been victorious.

Guard yourself from parasites that cling to you for your light and energy because they are thieves and robbers, they benefit more from being in your presence than you ever do or will from being in theirs As I mentioned earlier, you know a person by their fruit. Pick your fruit wisely.

Realize that the power they sap from you is the strength given to you by the Most High and his power is unlimited. Don't allow people who aren't willing to invest in your growth to rob you any longer. Unplug from people that empty your reserve tank and leave you empty. Learn to set boundaries and point them in the direction of one who can make all things new and who can also paint a masterpiece with a willing life. "For many are called, few are chosen." (Matt. 22:14)

The reason is that there is a you that others see that you haven't realized yet and the moment you do, a lot of people that have tried to keep you on the level of mediocrity know that they will be the first to be dismissed from your equation. So, they try to discourage you, talk about you and even cheer on bad choices to see how it will work out for you in the end.

Many have the ingredients to become the person they were created to be but none of them have the recipe to the making of you. Quit being on the menu when you are the table! There is only one you, love her and continue to walk in the confidence that you were designed for an awesome task... being you!

You Have a Life Song Sing It

"Wake up, Wake up, O Zion! Clothe yourself with strength…
Sit in a place of honor, Remove the chains of slavery from
your neck, O Captive Daughter of Zion"

(Isaiah 52:2)

The beauty of being who you are and were created to be amongst the thorns and weeds of life is such a liberating and refreshing evolution. When you observe nature, you will find no two flowers have the same pattern, no two zebras have the same stripe and neither do identical twins have the same fingerprints. In spite of all of the similarities twins have, they have different fingerprints and personalities. I speak from a family who has its share of twins. One particular set of twins, at birth, were hard to tell a part but their mother knew which one was which based on certain characteristics and their temperaments. Twins can share the same womb and sometimes split from the same ovum and be different. People may possess similarities but each person that exists is unique.

We are all designed to send out a different frequency and vibration into the atmosphere. One that creates the melody

231

that the Creator of the universe has perfectly orchestrated. Our lives are a masterpiece and a handiwork that has the Creator's autograph all over it, and when we are liberated by truth and walk in that liberty, it's a rhythm only one who has experienced it can explain. Your life becomes like a song I love by J. Moss, "Praise on the Inside." "There's a praise on the inside I can't keep to myself a holler stirring up from the depths of my soul, so excuse me if I seem a little silly or maybe even strange but praise is the way I say thanks."

In the days and what became weeks after losing my second oldest daughter, I realized that there truly is such a thing as living and just existing! My baby was just 26 years old but her life impacted people of all ages, and different social and economic levels. She was one that others woke up daily to see what she would say on social media; they watched her travels and how she dressed and cared for her children and how she and her husband loved each other. She was a hairstylist as well as an artist who, at a very young age, was at the top of her craft. She gave over the top, or as we would call them, extra birthday parties for her children as well as friends and family. My beloved was always ready to celebrate and would help you come up with a theme or color scheme to kick off the occasion. She was a dreamer and a visionary; these gifts are inspired by The Creator himself. My daughter had an infectious giggle that would turn into a hilarious cackle. She was fun, humorous, and if she liked you, she would protect you to a fault and even give you the shirt off of her back. She had a way of flashing her smile at you, you knew she loved you and she could shoot you a look also that would alert you to the fact that you want to stay clear of her.

I never imagined in a million years that I would be writing about her and her not being here because her cycle of living in time was up. Her legacy was supposed to be told by her children not myself, her mother. True enough, I am biased because she is mine, but I am also a handler of truth and if I couldn't say these things truthfully, I wouldn't have written this into my story at all. I spoke at her home going celebration and my charge to what seemed like over 500 or more people was to make sure that when you have to make this journey, the transition from time into eternity, that when the person has to stand and recall your life, it's the story you want told and not one they have to make up and lie about for you. Your life is a story and a song that sings about who you are. It's not what you say that speaks about who you are, but it is about what you do that speaks volumes about what you are made and comprised of.

Most people hear diminished chords and wonder why others question who they say they are, compared to what they see them do. Their two-step is all over the place and it is because what your life sings is all in a key that was never designed for you. You may have a note that was tampered with by the adversary because he knows that if you sang to the tune of your design, his power and the praise and worship he gets by robbing you of your joy and life song would be weakened. He can only hold you hostage as long as you obey his lies and twisted truth about liberation from truth being what makes you free and instrumental to the universe.

I mentioned earlier that everyone shouldn't have the privilege of speaking into your life, especially when they lived based on the beat of someone else's drum. A person should never be allowed to speak into your life if it doesn't come from a place of wisdom, love and experience. Wisdom comes from above according to scripture. "But the wisdom from above is first pure, then peaceable, gentle, open to reason, full of mercy and good fruits, impartial and sincere. And a harvest of righteousness is sown in peace by those who make peace." (James 3:17-18)

There is a chord only you are intended to sing to, and you have been set free to do so. Most of us waste a majority of our time doubting how capable we are of doing great things, but the truth is if we focused on the power that has been vested in us by the one who created us, we would be a force to be reckoned with. Vision and the ability to dream and bring forth something magnanimous is a gift placed in you by the Creator. "And afterward, I will pour out my Spirit on all people. Your sons and daughters will prophesy, your old men will dream dreams, your young men will see vision" (Joel 2:28)

But you can't do much if you aren't willing to walk the trodden out path. We can conquer giants just like David and interpret dreams like Joseph and Daniel.

"Joseph had a dream, and when he told it to his brothers, they hated him all the more. [6] He said to them, "Listen to this dream I had: [7] We were binding sheaves of grain out in the field when suddenly my sheaf rose and stood upright, while your sheaves gathered around mine and bowed down to it." His brothers said to him, "Do you intend to reign over us? Will you actually rule us?" And they hated him all the more because of his dream and what he had said." (Gen. 37:8-9)

"He reveals deep and hidden things; he knows what lies in darkness, and light dwells with him. I thank and praise you, Elohim of my ancestors: You have given me wisdom and power, you have made known to me what we asked of you, you have made known to us the dream of the king." Then Daniel went to Arioch, whom the king had appointed to execute the wise men of Babylon, and said to him, "Do not execute the wise men of Babylon. Take me to the king, and I will interpret his dream for him." (Dan. 2:22-24, 3:12)

How do I do this, live out my life song you may ask? I have discovered the formula. You ready? It's as simple as obeying the blue print of design, a universal principle that is the reason the earth still spins on its axis and the planets orbit in outer space, it's called obedience. Creation obeys the creator. You have to make a resolve about whom you will choose to obey. Will you trust and believe the truth of the set apart spirit that affirms to you that if you keep The Most Highs covenant, "Now if you obey me fully and keep my covenant, then out of all nations you will be my treasured possession. Although the whole earth is mine," (Exodus 19:5) or will you believe the lies about yourself that the enemy constantly tries to make you believe? The one whom you obey becomes your master.

The Sun was told to shine and it did, the Moon was told to give off light and it did "And Yah made two great lights; the greater light to rule the day, and the lesser light to rule the night: he made the stars also." (Genesis 1:16).

And we were created a little lower than the angels and walked in the garden with the Holy one until we did something opposite of what was commanded of us "Then Yah said, 'Let Us make man in Our image, according to Our likeness; let them have dominion over the fish of the sea, over the birds of the air, and over the cattle, over all the earth and over every creeping thing that creeps on the earth.' So, Yah created man in His *own* image; in the image of Elohim He created him; male and female He created them. Then Elohim blessed them, and Elohim said to them, 'Be fruitful and multiply; fill the earth and subdue it; have dominion over the fish of the sea, over the birds of the air, and over every living thing that moves on the earth.'" (Genesis 1:26-28)

And that's when all of the doubt, bondage and loss of harmony occurred. "Now the serpent was more cunning than any beast of the field which Yahua Elohim had made. And he said to the woman, 'Has Elohim indeed said, *You shall not eat of every tree of the garden*'?

And the woman said to the serpent, 'We may eat the fruit of the trees of the garden; but of the fruit of the tree which *is* in the midst of the garden, Elohim has said, *You shall not eat it, nor shall you touch it, lest you die.'*

Then the serpent said to the woman, 'You will not surely die. For Elohim knows that in the day you eat of it your eyes will be opened, and you will be like Elohim, knowing good and evil.'

So, when the woman saw that the tree *was* good for food, that it *was* pleasant to the eyes, and a tree desirable to make *one* wise, she took of its fruit and ate. She also gave to her husband with her, and he ate." (Genesis Chapter 3:1-6)

Our ancestors exchanged truth for a lie and have questioned the word of Yah from hence forth. Yah is always reminding us to be courageous and reminding us to trust Him . I have experienced victories beyond my imagination when I stopped seeing things through the lenses of my abilities. When I shifted to seeing the thought that there is more beyond the horizon that is possible and that Yah alone can roll back the veil of time and allow me to experience the glory of His majesty.

It seems to make no sense when you hear it, but 80% of our ability to function is because we have seen someone do certain things and we mimicked the action or behavior. If you nurture negative thoughts about your capacity to succeed, you will embrace the thoughts. However, if you subscribe to thinking on pure and lovely things encompassed in truth, you will experience a new evolution.

We marvel at the fact that Yeshua (who most of the world calls Jesus) was able to walk on water, heal, transcend space and time as well as perform miracles. The prophets of old and early disciples were able to raise the dead and break chains of bondage and it was because of their decision to be obedient to the word of their Creator. To hand the Most High their fears and inadequacies in exchange for His power and might. All of creation exists to testify of the truth of a supreme creator full of wisdom and love. We are given the very breath he breathed into the nostrils of man. Yah gave us the capacity to create , imagine and choose. Our life song can sing for him when we quit operation in discord and get on one accord with the song Yah placed in our heart to sing back to him. You are different; a descendant of the most capable one created to proclaim His glory. I can't wait to hear your song!

Beauty from Brokenness

Stop Picking Up Strays

If it's one thing that I have learned from being disappointed it is that you should quit trying to bring others where you are being elevated to. Some places are only meant for you to elevate to and what is meant for you is for you. Trying to bring a person to a place that they aren't ready for can become an agonizing feat of tug a war. When it is all said and done, the one you are trying to drag to higher ground will resent you for trying to make them come where they aren't ready to go. You may end up despising them for wasting your time because they were comfortable where they were before you came trying to take them higher. Pigs love pig pens and snakes like to hide under rocks, people who are givers by nature always believe they can love or nurture a person enough for them to desire to be elevated, but the truth is there are only two kinds of people in this world, givers and takers. Sometimes you can want more for a person than they want for themselves. Some people are looking for someone to do all of the work so that they can benefit from it but never had any intention on participating. They are just along for the ride until you run out of fuel.

Not walking with your equal is a recipe for conflict and strife. "Can two walk together unless they agreed to do so?" (Amos 3:3)

Elevation happens when you have been obedient with the first assignment you have been entrusted with. You don't necessarily have to be perfect or the best at getting it done but you do have to be available, willing and obedient. The Most High will not trust you with the next assignment or truth until you obey the first one. If he tells you to leave a particular place, or a certain circle of friends, flee.

This scripture always rings true when I am challenged with whether or not I should try and bring someone along the road that Yahweh has revealed to me. Vision only comes when you are connected to the one who orchestrated the entire plan. The reason being is the principle of the universe is reciprocity. Everything that is put here contributes to the universe and how it was designed to function. Trees give oxygen and take carbon monoxide out of the atmosphere, deposit a seed in soil, it produces that which you planted, parasites and certain kinds of people that I call takers will attach themselves to you as their source, but never give anything back. They will become bigger and stronger than you because they are depleting you of nutrients and they will slow you down because what has been deposited into you to accomplish your mission is only for you. Also, because parasites are only as strong as their host and the source the host is connected to; they are robbers of nutrients and time. The saddest thing about having a taker or a parasite is that either we stay too long in an unfavorable place and they attached themselves to us or we invited them along for the ride against all clear understanding. We often have the tendency to see the good and potential in others that they fail to see in themselves and we want to nurture them or elevate them to the same position we are in because we believe that they would benefit from where we are going, and we could make a good team. Not! Know why? Because, parasites can only take! You wind up becoming an accessory to their very existence and happiness was never part of the plan and you wind up depleted, empty and miserable! I was raised not allowing others to borrow my clothes. My great aunts and aunties were excellent seamstresses, so they made me outfits out of leftover material from projects they had completed. I remember this particular time I wanted a jersey fitted skirt and top, these were popular in the late 80s. I was in the 9th grade. The outfit was worn with a double belt and ruffled sock and oxfords. I had to have one! My aunt Bertha made me a pattern for the outfit out of newspaper and helped me sew it . I made this yellow skirt set and I was proud of my handiwork. At school there was a girl that shared classes with me and I thought she was a friend, later to find out she wasn't. Anyway, she asked to wear my outfit to a dance and against what I had been taught: "You don't let people borrow your things, especially clothes," I obliged her. I loaned this girl my handmade outfit that was tailored just for me and she wore it to the party. I did this against all of the things I knew about her physical and personal hygiene. Meaning she wasn't a very clean person as far as personal hygiene. She wore makeup, curled her hair and even put on perfume. The perfume often seemed like it was sprayed on to cover the failure to bathe or wash her clothes. I know, why did I do it? I am a person that values a person's trust, so if you entrust me with something, I will return it better than how you gave it to me. I learned a valuable lesson because after the weekend when the outfit was due back it wasn't returned. I asked for it numerous times only be given the run around. I found out that my outfit was being passed around. Her older sister had borrowed it and she was in high school. She left the top at a friend's house she had stayed with the weekend she wore the outfit. So, what seemed like a whole four weeks of getting the runaround about my attire, the girl I loaned the outfit to comes to school with my what used to be bright yellow skirt set on. I was infuriated when I saw her at breaktime wearing a dingy yellow skirt set that resembled mine! I couldn't believe my eyes! Instead of returning my outfit like she promised she would or even trying to restore it to its original quality, she wore it. Wore it knowing I would see it ruined. This ended in a verbal confrontation that almost got physical. I would adopt the concept that I don't loan my clothes out and stick to it. Now if it's something that I have worn or it holds no sentimental value to me, I will allow the person to have what it is they ask to wear. Nonetheless, as I was writing this principle, this story reminded me about what happened when I picked up a stray "friend" she took advantage of my generosity and squandered what was something I took great pride in producing.

Getting rid of "strays" or "parasites," I have literally had to cut them off and in some instances, I have literally had to stop and play dead long enough for the leech to detach and look for another host. On the flip side, playing dead and stopping held up my arrival time to my designated location. But as I stated before, what is for you is for you. By the grace of the Most High I arrived with a lesson and experience in tow.

Setting firm boundaries is very necessary for you to regain your strength and focus. Learning to forgive myself for being foolish and disobeying as well as deviating so far off the plan that Yah had for me has been fundamental in my healing and growth.

So many times, my ETA has been delayed because I have tried to bring someone along on my journey. You cannot bring a person to a destination Yah has tailor-made for you especially when they are in total opposition to the work of your creator. I have tried to bring along strays that didn't understand the heart of my Master. This is why they were not in agreement with where I was going. So, what ended up happening is, I became disobedient to the Creator and found myself on a walk in the wilderness, disappointed and open to the attacks of my adversaries because I chose to deposit what was for me into a person who either by design or by choice has decided to not participate. And what I later discovered was they deny the very power that the creator possesses.

Sometimes you have to run for cover and come back for the wounded when you're strong enough to lead them out without being wounded yourself. And other times you just have to move forward and not look back.

You can't drive forward looking in the rearview mirror, a wreck is bound to happen.

Quit acquiescing to a lifestyle that is too low to contain your presence just because a person desires your presence doesn't mean they are ready for you! Or should be allowed to dwell in yours.

Frenemy

Ever heard your words repeated back to you or been invited to a party, dinner etc., to be surrounded by a group of women that know more about you then you've ever divulged to them? I mean the only person you all have in common is the one that invited you all and she seemed genuine when you vented about your child's behavior at school, or when you were upset after discovering your teenage daughter was pregnant, or when you and your mate or significant other were experiencing a rough patch. Yes, we have all fallen victim of a frenemy, one who seems concerned, sincere and fun to be around to later discover you trusted a mean girl! This is a subject my heart felt compelled to address. Uncovering and exposing is such an ugly practice but many people have been subjected to this act. To act, to me, is the ultimate act of betrayal in my opinion.

I stand behind a salon chair for 8 to 16 hours a day most of my week, and I've done this for the last 24 years and, contrary to popular belief, salons aren't what television depicts. They always portray a place where there is fighting, gossip and all other sorts of foolery! I don't know how others are running their businesses out there, but in most salons, relationships are built, and you become acquainted and very intimate with your stylist. It's a very personal environment. Not only do I get to touch you, your head, or face but I touch your life and vice versa. My clients share parts of their lives with me and in exchange I transform their looks, as well as mood and I see a dimension only trusted few are privy to. Some people open the curtains to the windows of their souls to me, they let me see their joy, and pain. I am allowed to share births weddings, sorrow or the loss of life. I even prepare some of my clients shells for their families to have final closure. I see marriages and I see the betrayal of vows. I speak to the one who is struggling with what love is as well as the one who is stuck in the perpetual cycle of looking for love in all the wrong places. I pray for my clients as well as have them pray for me. I come in contact periodically with those whose actions spew hate and malice and hurt others' feelings as well. Those don't last long though because light contrasts and pushes darkness out. I see arguments on the web and people exposing one another's pain or taking stabs at their character, but the only way they have the ammunition to do so is because they were trusted with the privilege of information being divulged to them and they don't possess the quality of a real friend.

Yes! I'm a vault for other people's decompression, hurt and pain, and it can be overwhelming and grievous at times, but you know what would be detrimental to my character and the title friend that I don't take lightly? The detrimental thing would be to diminish my integrity and their trust and expose them just to suit another person's insatiable eagerness to know what they have entrusted unto me. I'm not tooting my own horn, just simply speaking from the vantage point of being the one that has allowed others in my vault to only discover that they were pirates! Only there to scout out enough treasure to expose me.

These encounters caused me to desire to be the friend that I see others not capable of being. Being a friend and having one is a blessing and privilege. I always refer to my friendship as a circle and a circle is symbolic to eternity; it has no breaks or gaps in it, a circle can grow larger or smaller, but the circle still exists. Every now and then a Judas will be in the camp, but they expose and remove themselves. See, Judas liked the position and benefits of being in the Master's presence but only to be noticed, he cared nothing about the fact that Yeshua (Jesus) loved him. Judas had an agenda; he was the treasurer and only had interest in the money. And If you read the text, he hung himself. (Matt. 27:1-10)

This should cause us all to evaluate why we seek friendships. I hold friendship at a very high value and am careful about who I consider a friend. It's very endearing to me that others trust me with their innermost concerns and share a piece of their lives with me. I don't take this privilege lightly because I hold family, friendship and loyalty at a very high regard.

A "frenemy" is a portmanteau of "friend" and "enemy" that can refer to either an enemy pretending to be a friend or someone who really is a friend but also a rival. You've heard the cliché: "Keep your friends close and your enemies closer!" Let's talk about frenemies and see if you don't change your mind about the company you keep. Most crimes that involve blunt objects or knives happen to be done by someone the victim knew or trusted. Who was it that betrayed Jesus and sold him for 30 pieces of silver to be crucified? Judas, one of the 12 disciples; however, scripture says he was the son of perdition. (John 17:12) Meaning a person with an unredeemable soul or utter destruction, eternally damned. Although he was chosen, he allowed his heart to be controlled by the Devil to result in his eternal separation from Yeshua. Then we have Gaius Cassius Longinus and his brother-in-law Marcus Junius Brutus who were very close to Caesar Augustus who along with 40 others stabbed him to death after his friend Brutus greeted him with a kiss. A friend sticks closer than a brother and is born for times of adversity not to create havoc and bring down wrath for you! A friend is a person that has your greater good in mind and seeks your best interest. A talebearer reveals secrets and exposes your hurt and embarrassment because of their need to control the narrative. We of the female species start in daycare and on play dates sizing up each other and deciding who we are going to play with or if we will invite a specific girl to our birthday party. Even down to letting them sit with us at lunch only to shun them or throw shade or make her uncomfortable. Friends are supposed to encourage and build one another up, they protect one another emotionally and physically and always do what's in the greater good of the friend.

Talebearers or gossipers are dangerous, as they whisper, reveal, and kill characters and relationships. This is a decisive and wicked character trait. The Devil whispers and divides humanity and creates discord and when you practice uncovering and exposing others' secrets, you participate in the agenda of the evil one the adversary, accuser. With a more high-tech world things aren't just whispered in a phone conversation, now a whisper can be heard around the globe in one click. I hear women speak about how they allowed others in their circle to only become the victim of a frenemy! Poor choices in who we trust can have a negative effect. We should be just as prayerful about the people we desire to entertain as prayerful as you would be about choosing a spouse. There are friends who destroy each other, but a real friend sticks closer than a brother. (NLT Proverbs 18:24) We are supposed to be the kind of friend that we would like someone to be to us, we must show ourselves friendly, reliable and trustworthy.

Repetition makes the master to become good at anything, you must practice, so to be mean and divisive you put in as much time as you would being dependable and trustworthy. The world and all the unrealistic images that are thrown our way as young women and women period is enough to send you into a tizzy. Society and media do enough exposing love and friendship in a foolish and twisted way. How about we shake up and wake up some of our fellow queens and show them what the true beauty of being and having a friend is really about? Remember, you get back what you deposit in this life, let's plant some seeds that will grow fruit that we don't mind eating or sharing. Remember I am on a curse reversing mission.

#KeepinItRoyal

Looking in My Rearview

As I reflect on my former years, I have realized that I don't have to stay anywhere that causes me pain and that strangles my growth. I have always felt like the butterfly that never gets to emerge from her chrysalis without someone knocking on her cocoon before it is time to emerge. This year, I chose to allow a lot of suppressed feelings and emotions to come forth. I chose to break loose and be. Every time I emerge, I am better, wiser and spiritually stronger, and might I add, more multifaceted than before!

The lesson I've learned is there will always be noise and interference but push past it, it's only a test. Someone is always watching and waiting to give a report; whether it be positive or negative, guard your truth. I've learned that a half-truth is still a lie and that people will believe a half-truth faster than they will believe a whole truth. I have experienced people that hate you will say they love you and the ones that think they hate you only feel that way because they lack the courage to stand out. People will deflect the really hate themselves onto you because it doesn't take a lot of energy to focus on themselves then it takes to critique you and your elevation. Change requires being intentional and intentionality can be scary to people who are accustomed to living haphazardly. Growing means pressing past the seeds of doubt and failure that have been dropped in people's minds. 1

I've learned that a lie will spread faster than truth and that people love to dine on the shitty little morsels covered in gravy and salt and pepper and become full from eating what isn't even sustainable. It's waste covered in flour, oil, salt, pepper and water. I've learned that you can learn a lot from another person's shortcomings. People can't wait to believe the worst about you and will go to drastic measures to prove what is false is true and will never take the time to research or investigate truth.

I know that only I am accountable for what I have done with the Most High's gifts, talents and word.

I have learned, although many watch, my real audience is the maker of heaven and earth.

"I know I never lose, either I win, or I learn a lesson." ~Nia Marie

Let the King Resurrect You

"And he took the damsel by the hand, and said unto her,
Talitha cumi; which is, being interpreted, little girl, I say unto
thee, arise."

(Mark 5:41)

In the beginning of this chapter, Yeshua and his disciples are coming back from a boat ride where they witnessed the king of the world speak to a raging storm and it ceases. After they reach the town east of the Jordon called Gardarenos, they encounter a man tormented with a legion of demons that have full control over this man's ability to reason. But after an encounter with Yeshua, the possessed man is clothed in his right mind. On His next excursion, Yeshua is met by one of the religious rulers of the synagogue, his name is Jairus. Jairus was in great despair because his daughter was sick unto the point of death. The ruler who was in charge of the arrangement of the temple realized that he needed the masters help.

He fell at Yeshua's feet and begged Yeshua to lay hands on his daughter and heal her. Yeshua charged him not to fear and agreed to go heal his daughter. Many in the community followed after Yeshua to witness another one of his miraculous healings. On the way to Jairus's house, many bumped and touched him in the crowd, but one particular touch caught his attention. A woman who had an issue that no doctor could heal spoke in her heart and said that if she could just touch the hem of his garment, she knew she could be healed. And out of all of the friction and touches from those in the crowd, Yeshua acknowledges this touch. Behind this touch was faith and purpose. This woman chose to pursue the master for an experience. Out of the many that were following him to see what he would do at the house for Jairus's daughter, this woman wanted to have an intimate encounter of her own. She didn't want to talk about what she would see him do for someone else, but she wanted to have a personal story to tell. Yeshua told her that her faith and her choice to believe in the power he possessed was what made her whole.

Jairus' daughter had her father and his faith in the master advocating on her behalf. She would be dead from her illness by the time Yeshua would reach her father's house. This didn't intimidate Yeshua one bit. He allowed his closest disciples to witness what he would do as well as the girl's mother and father. Yeshua took the girl by her hand and commanded her to arise! He gave this girl who was only 12 at the time a new lease on life. Where sickness had overtaken her and robbed her of what looked like the rest of her life, Yeshua commanded death to release her.

The master of the universe has the same power today to command life over the things we believe are impossible. We will just give him our dead situations. The beauty of what Yeshua can do with a life fully surrendered and that has chosen to allow him to do the work is above anything you can hope or imagine. In this story, the young girl had succumbed to sickness and had no choice in her demise. But in his love and compassion, Yeshua restored wholeness to those who couldn't advocate for themselves.

In many of life's trials, I have tried to resuscitate dead marriages, friendships and business deals. In my refusal to let go, I missed a lot of the beauty of allowing the king of the universes' healing hand.

After all that I have chosen to do against my better judgement, I am so grateful that Yeshua didn't write me off. I am humbled that the king of the universe has allowed my failures to be resurrected to glorify Him. I was reminded that the prayers of my elders and love ones before me are still a frequency in the universe that have also met me on my journey. These prayers have sustained me when I didn't know better and when I wasn't trusting The Most High for the outcome. The prayers Yeshua answered that were sent ahead for me when I had lost my way sustained and kept me. Today, I stand on my own truths and intimate experiences. Yeshua still takes little girls by the hand and command them to "arise." The word in Hebrew is a verb (koom) which literally means to stand up, stand, be confirmed. This word requires action! I have come to believe that if you have endured and overcome adversity this was not done so that you could waste time singing the blues about what you have been through. Yah sustained you so that just like Jairus and the man with the legion of demons, and the woman with the issue of blood, you can testify of his power.

In life, I have believed the lies in my head. The ones that have held me hostage from being healed and testifying to another that they can be capable and whole. The lies that I'm the only one that has been through what I have experienced. This was not true. Yah allowed me to be made whole to help carry another over the threshold of their darkest hour. He has sustained me to encourage someone that beauty can emerge from situations that look impossible.

Take the king's hand, arise and stand in his truth.

As I Think so am I!

"Life and death are in the power of the tongue, and as a man thinketh so his he." Proverbs 18:21, Proverbs 23:7, "Out of the abundance of your heart the mouth speaks."

(Matthew 12:34)

Elevate.

You are too big for already manufactured circles.

It is high time you customize your own excellence. You are no longer an accessory to someone else's happiness, you are the table where it all dwells. It's imperative that you become the one who is offering the seats. The phrase sticks and stones may break my bones, but words will never hurt me must have been a deaf man's truth!

Words are powerful, they have the ability to build you up or tear you down. Words can cause you to believe and achieve great things or words can hold you prisoner.

And no words are more powerful than the ones we recite in our own mind.

As a man thinks so is he.

If I don't meditate and ruminate on what is positive, I can edify lies and perpetuate my own demise.

See, I get so sick of people proclaiming to be real and all they speak is ignorance and negativity, the things they say may very well be true or their truth but if it causes destruction, what was the purpose for releasing the negative vibrations into the atmosphere?

It is a proven fact that we possess the power to create, shape and manifest our thoughts into words, and our words into deeds, by way of creating a physical manifestation of a simple thought or emotion.

Many may argue about what the Creator's name is or if a supreme one exists but we all can agree that there is a Creator, and with a vibration, or as I believe with a spoken language and voice the universe and the inhabitants came to be.

With love, and purpose all came to exists. You can't say that the vibration that created the splendor of space, time and the depths of the sea wasn't one of love.

Or that the one who so meticulously arraigned the complexity of the brain and organs wasn't careful about how he arraigned his thoughts.

Because everything here was created to work harmonious and in sync. What greater evidence of what words spoken can do?

The manuscript that I study said in Gen. 1:26, "And Yahua said, 'Let us make man in our image, after our likeness: and let them have dominion over the fish of the sea, and over the fowl of the air, and over the cattle, and over all the earth, and over every creeping thing that creepeth upon the earth.' So Yahua created man in his *own* image, in the image of Yahua created he him; male and female created he them."

A single thought with love and purpose created, right?

Now fathom this; if we are created in His likeness and with the same attributes as our creator except for omnipotence, omniscience, and omnipresence, our positive and negative thoughts can bring forth purpose.

We have the ability to reason, choose, produce life, create a positive or negative environment in which we live.

"Can't make a silk purse out of a pig skin!" Same goes with words; you cannot produce positive results with negative thoughts and deeds. Remove negative people from your circle.

The road less traveled may not be filled with your peers but it sure is one filled with peace, joy and blessings.

Obedience opened doors to places and opportunities that you couldn't even imagine.

"Meekness does not allow the mind to run away with vain imaginations and to dwell on thoughts which inflame volatile emotions and passion." (2 Cor. 10:3-5; Philippians 4:8-9)

The rash woman is filled with suspicions, doubts, and assumptions based entirely on emotion, and allows these imaginations to determine the course of action. Keep your mind on pure and lovely things. "Finally, brothers and sisters, whatever is true, whatever is noble, whatever is right, whatever is pure, whatever is lovely, whatever is admirable—if anything is excellent or praiseworthy—think about such things. Whatever you have learned or received or heard from me or seen in me—put it into practice. And the Yahuah of peace will be with you." (Philippians 4:8)

About the Author

Nia M. Hodge-Grier's focal point has always been from an artistic lens. Nia has been in the beauty industry for 25 years. She has mastered making others beautiful to the naked eye, but during life's journey noticed that beauty runs deeper than the exterior. Nia has evolved and faced different adversities in life and realized that ministering to the whole woman was the most important element in being beautiful. Nia has gleaned and learned from women, being transparent in her chair and from them sharing their troubles and some of her own that healing was needed to be a whole woman. Nia lives in the central valley where she was born and raised. Nia is the mother of five children: three daughters and two sons. Nia also has 11 grandchildren: six boys, five girls. Nia loves to cook, sew, read and write. Nia is also the author of *Food for Life* a cookbook for healthy food alternatives. Nia has a community garden in southwest Fresno named Inside Out Community Garden. Nia also runs a non-profit in memory of her daughter and granddaughter The Hive Asthma Awareness Foundation.

Made in the USA
Columbia, SC
17 October 2020

22998894R00167